UNSHAKABLE

D1413096

UNSHAKABLE

STANDING FIRM IN A SHIFTING CULTURE

K. SCOTT OLIPHINT AND ROD MAYS

PUBLISHING
P.O. BOX 817 • PHILLIPSBURG • NEW JERSEY 08865-0817

Library of Congress Cataloging-in-Publication Data

Names: Oliphint, K. Scott, 1955- author. | Mays, Rod, 1950-
Title: Unshakable : standing firm in a shifting culture / K. Scott Oliphint, Rod Mays.
Other titles: Things that cannot be shaken
Description: P&R Publishing edition. | Phillipsburg : P&R Publishing, 2016. | Rev. ed. of: Things that cannot be shaken : holding fast to your faith in a relativistic world. c2008. | Includes bibliographical references.
Identifiers: LCCN 2016001114| ISBN 9781629951607 (pbk.) | ISBN 9781629951614 (epub) | ISBN 9781629951621 (mobi)
Subjects: LCSH: Christian life. | Christianity and culture. | Theology, Doctrinal.
Classification: LCC BV4501.3 .O465 2016 | DDC 248.4--dc23
LC record available at http://lccn.loc.gov/2016001114

To John Weiser—one of Zion's children

GLORIOUS things of thee are spoken,
Zion, city of our God!
He, whose word cannot be broken,
Form'd thee for his own abode.
On the Rock of Ages founded,
What can shake thy sure repose?
With salvation's walls surrounded,
Thou may'st smile at all thy foes.

See! the streams of living waters
Springing from eternal love,
Well supply thy sons and daughters,
And all fear of want remove:
Who can faint, while such a river
Ever flows their thirst t'assuage?
Grace, which, like the Lord, the giver,
Never fails from age to age.

Round each habitation hovering,
See the cloud and fire appear!
For a glory and a covering,
Showing that the Lord is near:
Thus deriving from their banner
Light by night, and shade by day;
Safe they feed upon the manna
Which he gives them when they pray.

Bless'd inhabitants of Zion,
Wash'd in the Redeemer's blood!
Jesus, whom their souls rely on,
Makes them kings and priests to God:
'Tis his love his people raises
Over self to reign as kings,
And as priests his solemn praises
Each for a thank-offering brings.

Saviour, if of Zion's city
I through grace a member am;
Let the world deride or pity,
I will glory in thy name:
Fading is the worldling's pleasure,
All his boasted pomp and show;
Solid joys and lasting treasure,
None but Zion's children know.

CONTENTS

Preface   11

1. Says Who?   17
   He Whose Word Cannot Be Broken

2. Our Deepest Need   45
   See! The Streams of Living Waters

3. We Are Not Alone   73
   Round Each Habitation Hovering

4. Payment and Punishment   103
   Washed in the Redeemer's Blood!

5. Seeing the Unseen   129
   Solid Joys and Lasting Treasure

PREFACE

There is something compelling about the life stories of people who have been radically changed by God. The "this-is-what-I-was-but-this-is-what-I-am-now" stories capture our attention. Perhaps this captivation is due to an understanding of the power of sin in our lives and the hope of the power of the gospel.

In Romans chapters 7 and 8, the apostle Paul shares his all-consuming struggle with sin. By the middle of chapter 8, Paul turns his attention to describing his hope in the work of the Holy Spirit in spite of his constant struggle with sin. This assurance of God's redeeming work in Paul's life is grounded in the cross of Christ. Paul's struggle, his circumstances, do not define his position before God. His position before God is founded in the obedient life and death of Christ his Savior. At the end of Romans 8, Paul writes with certainty about the ultimate victory he will enjoy, when his life is consummated in glory. Paul's experience, from Romans 7–8, reminds us of the "bookends" of the normal Christian life. Throughout the believer's experience, daily circumstances lead him to cry out with Paul, "Wretched man that I am! Who will deliver me from this body of death?" (Rom. 7:24). How sweet to be able to contemplate the truth of Jesus' work in the middle of the struggle: "Who shall separate us from the love of Christ?" (Rom. 8:35).

One of the great "this-is-what-I-was" stories is that of John Newton. His transformation from vile slave trader to Anglican minister and hymn writer is well known by now. One of his best-known hymns, "Glorious Things of Thee Are Spoken," has served as the inspiration for this book. This hymn encourages believers to remember God's protection of his people. He will never fail us. He will guide and provide for us, all because we have been "washed in the Redeemer's blood."

John Newton was born July 24, 1725, in London. His mother taught him the Bible but died when he was seven. His father seemed uninterested in rearing his son. Newton spent his early life as a sailor and slave trader. He was miraculously converted during a storm at sea. After his conversion, he attempted to continue in the slave trade and tried to restrain its inherent evils in his own practices. He eventually quit sailing and was ordained in the Anglican Church. Newton took a parish in the village of Olney. He later met William Cowper, a poet who had moved to Olney. Cowper's life was marked by periods of severe depression. Newton took Cowper into his home on several occasions when it became difficult for Cowper to live alone. Newton was a pastor to Cowper, encouraging Cowper to write hymns based on his suffering and his awareness of God's work during these difficult times in Cowper's life. The hymns of Newton and Cowper (a collection of approximately three hundred) became known as the Olney Hymns. Some 233 of these compositions are attributed to Newton.

Newton's hymns, such as "Amazing Grace," "I Asked the Lord," and "How Sweet the Name of Jesus Sounds," contain obvious references to his own profound understanding of sin in the human heart. His appreciation for his unworthiness of God's love, as well as his gratefulness for the pardoning grace of God, finds clear expression in all his writings. It was this understanding of God's grace and his own sinfulness that led him to show such compassion to Cowper.

Newton's perception of the pervasiveness of his own sin caused the cross to be an immeasurably large factor in his life. It was said of Newton, "He believes and feels his own weakness and unworthiness and lives upon the grace and pardoning love of his Lord. This gives him an habitual tenderness and gentleness of spirit."[1] John Newton was a faithful husband to Mary for forty years. He died December 21, 1807, at the age of eighty-two. He continues to speak to us today through his hymns.

Hymns are alternately defined as songs of praise or spiritual songs. By definition, their purpose is to tell the story of redemption. Older hymns connect us with the past as we see how Christians from earlier generations applied the gospel to their lives in times of wandering, struggling, disappointment or joy, and celebration. Newton's hymns are rich with theology. In the preface to the Olney Hymns, he wrote, "The views I have received of the doctrines of grace are essential to my peace; I could not live comfortably a day or an hour without them. I likewise believe . . . them to be friendly to holiness and to have a direct influence in producing and maintaining a gospel conversation; and therefore, I must not be ashamed of them."[2] Newton also stated, "The scripture which teaches us what we are to say is equally explicit as to the temper and spirit in which we are to speak. Though I had knowledge of all mysteries, and the tongue of an angel to declare them, I could hope for little acceptance or usefulness, unless I was to speak in love."[3]

1. Richard Cecil, "Memoirs of the Reverend John Newton," in *The Works of the Reverend John Newton* (Edinburgh: Banner of Truth, 1985), 170.
2. John Newton, *The Works of the Reverend John Newton* (Edinburgh: Banner of Truth, 1985), 3:303.
3. Ibid., 5:131.

Newton describes the Christian life with refreshing honesty in his hymns. He does not engage in sugarcoating, sanitizing, or romanticizing the believer's experience in an effort to communicate a pious, stoic response to daily struggles. Through his hymns, Newton speaks directly to our experience, allowing us to see his own joy and sorrow in trials and sufferings, his life of learning the reality of faith. His hymn, "I Asked the Lord," captures this thought:

> I asked the Lord that I might grow in faith and love and
>   every grace,
> Might more of His salvation know and seek more earnestly
>   His face.
> 'Twas He who taught me thus to pray, and He I trust has
>   answered prayer,
> But it has been in such a way as almost drove me to despair.
> I hoped that in some favored hour at once He'd answer my
>   request,
> And by His love's constraining power subdue my sins and
>   give me rest.
>
> Instead of this, He made me feel the hidden evils of my
>   heart,
> And let the angry powers of hell assault my soul in every part.
> Yea, more with His own hand He seemed intent to aggravate
>   my woe,
> Crossed all the fair designs I schemed, cast out my feelings,
>   laid me low.
>
> Lord, why is this, I trembling cried, Wilt Thou pursue Thy
>   worm to death?
> "'Tis in this way," the Lord replied, "I answer prayer for grace
>   and faith."

"These inward trials I employ from self and pride to set
    thee free
And break thy schemes of earthly joy that thou mayest seek
    thy all in me."

These beautiful words show Christians what it means to be honest about our sin. Consequently, these hymns do not encourage Christian pretense, as if our salvation means that we are better people in and of ourselves. They do not erect barriers to unbelievers, who resent piously pretentious hypocrisy. Because these hymns are grounded in Scripture, the words transcend the sometimes popular idea that the church and God are not relevant. The poetic language both connects us to the past and speaks to our present circumstances.

Following Newton's example, how do we love those who are suffering? What can we communicate to them with that habitual tenderness and gentleness of spirit that characterized John Newton's love? How do we show compassion to those whose marriages are falling apart? How do we encourage parents of rebellious, difficult children? What do we say to those who are overwhelmed with the problem of too little money, or too much? Is there tenderness and compassion in our voices and attitudes when we talk to others about their sexual confusion, addiction to pornography, or chemical substances? Are we patient and loving to those who suffer from depression and disappointment, who may be victims of their own sin or the sins of others? What is the basis for the hope we can give?

What guides us and informs our answers, both for others and for ourselves? "He, whose word cannot be broken," helps us think through the answers. How does the gospel impact the way we engage other people? "See! the streams of living waters springing from eternal love . . ."; we love others as we have been loved. How can I rest in Christ? "Safe they feed upon the manna, which he gives them when they pray . . ."; prayer brings rest and peace as we acknowledge that only Jesus can help. What does faith in Christ look like as we struggle against the power of sin? "Washed in the Redeemer's blood . . ."; that promise gives the hope of future glory with Christ. What shapes my relationships? "Fading is the worldling's pleasure, all his boasted pomp and show." Genuine love is selfless, and motivated by gratitude for the redemption we have received in the Son.

As Newton's great hymn—and the gospel truths of Scripture that lie behind it—provides the backdrop of this book, our hope is that we will, together, be encouraged to set aside those sins that cling so closely. In the midst of a world sometimes overly enamored with the new and with change, we hope that those "things that cannot be shaken" (Heb. 12:27) will become our only hope, that in the words of Newton, "solid joys and lasting treasure" will become the defining character of our walk with Christ.

1: SAYS WHO?

HE WHOSE WORD CANNOT BE BROKEN

Glorious things of thee are spoken,
Zion, city of our God!
He, whose word cannot be broken,
Form'd thee for his own abode.
On the Rock of Ages founded,
What can shake thy sure repose?
With salvation's walls surrounded,
Thou may'st smile at all thy foes.

THE QUESTION OF AUTHORITY

Today's young adults face some special challenges.[1] Whatever the proper label—whether postmodern, postconservative, or posteverything—the ideas and beliefs of popular culture have so inundated life in this world that such ideas and beliefs can all too easily become a natural part of our thinking and living. A college student on a typical campus today has learned the cultural drill well: "Doubt everything taught by anyone; submit your ideas

---

1. What we use as a label for these young adults—Generation X? Millennials?—is not terribly important, in part, because it is inexact, and, in part, because what we say here really applies to all of us.

to no authority." To fail to doubt is to fail to be heard. Perhaps no demographic in the history of our country has been fed a daily diet so heavy in tolerance and inclusiveness and so light in truth as these newer generations have. Any form of authority exists to be challenged, ignored, and likely rejected. To accept the ultimate authority of any person, document, or institution is to be bigoted, intolerant, unloving, and self-righteous.

The conventional wisdom dictates that we view the drama of life played out around us with a combination of cynicism, skepticism, and suspicion. In a context of such confusion, it is hard to convince oneself of what is real, or really important. We have been taught to take hold of our own destinies and to create our own reality. In far too many cases, we have attempted to do exactly this—and seen disastrous results.

The newer generations living in the twenty-first century have never known what life is like without television or videocassette/CD/DVD recorders or TiVo. Because of technology, we can, at least in some sense, "create" the reality we desire. It is now possible, for example, to program electronic screens with what we want to see when we want to see it. We can use preselected iPod tunes as the soundtrack for our lives. This has the double effect of, on the one hand, creating the feelings and ambience we desire, and on the other hand, letting the rest of the world go by.

In this kind of environment, many of the new generation say they believe in Christianity, that they trust God and his Word, but become tongue-tied, embarrassed, or defensive when their beliefs are questioned or challenged. Not only so, the notion of a universal authority that applies to one and all is almost completely foreign to the contemporary context. The authority of Christ and his Word is acceptable at the personal level perhaps, but it is almost a foregone conclusion that it cannot be applied to everyone.

Not too long ago, a group of students (twentysomethings) gathered for a Bible study. The speaker had spent a fair amount of time discussing the authority and truth of the Bible with these self-professed Christian believers. Near the end of the meeting, group members began to ask questions: But what about the Qur'an? What about the Book of Mormon? How do the findings of numerology or "historical facts" contained in other ancient documents affect the authority of the Bible? Is there really only one way to God? Are not all religions just different ways of saying the same thing? Why should we believe the Bible's claims over the claims of other religions? There seems to be a significant gap in the ability of most today to synthesize the truth of the Bible with what we see around us. Because of this inability, the Bible is reduced to the level of helpful personal advice and inspirational thought.

The problem posed in reconciling biblical truth with apparent contradictions in experience, of course, is the problem of authority. This problem is not a new one. And the questions that come today have their central focus in the question of truth and authority. The focus of the question may change in different periods of history, but the basic question is always the same: To whom or what should I ultimately submit? How can I know what is true and what is not?

AUTHORITY'S SOURCES

It may come as no surprise to students of history, especially the history of thought, that in today's confused climate two primary views on the source of truth or authority emerge. People seem to believe either that truth is what makes them feel good and works best with their experience (which is sometimes labeled *empiricism*) or that truth is what makes sense to them objectively and intellectually (which is sometimes labeled *rationalism*). Are either of these approaches acceptable in developing and nurturing a system of truth and a notion of authority?

If It Feels Good . . .

Empiricism is, by definition, the obtaining of knowledge through the senses, or through experience. Right experiences will bring an understanding of truth—or so we think. These experiences, both emotional and physical, are often defined by the popular media that inundate today's generation, including music, television, film, and poetry. Media of this kind can create an ambience of authority because they tell stories in ways that are appealing. In music, the stories are told with a particular mood or beat, making them easy to remember and repeat. In television or film, they are told with images, visual art and effects, and musical score, all of which combine to capture imaginations and promote ideas and worldviews. In most cases, however, the stories told, the images produced, and the effects desired have their sources in just another human emotion, experience, or desire. It can be tempting to commit oneself to a particular song's or movie's "message." But these messages themselves only go as deep as the individual(s) who produced them.

If history teaches us anything, it is that human beings are not particularly good at defining their own happiness. We are not adept at articulating clearly what it is we really want. Some of what we think we want may be good; we may think what we want is simply the absence of conflict with other humans or the absence of conflict within ourselves. But even if these goals are good ones, the solutions offered may not be. Remedies offered for getting rid of these conflicts—things like more money, more time, fewer responsibilities, more autonomy, or maybe just the ability to have the ultimate makeover (of home, hair, teeth, or brain)—are all supposed to provide what we need. If they provide for our needs producing less conflicted lives, they must give us truth.

In keeping with the empirical, some may base their lives on what they "feel" like doing at any given time. They may not feel like going to class, or studying, or going to work. In seeking to orchestrate the right feelings, we may seek to change the atmosphere (music, entertainment, activity), the location (new city, new apartment, new bed), the vocation, or the surrounding family (spouse, parents, siblings) and friends (new significant other, new group, or new church). Change may create a sense of busyness and thus a distraction from reality, an escape from the everyday grind, and an illusion of self-created happiness.

But isn't distraction really just a means of escape? We turn up the music and get lost in the melody and the words, hoping that the pain and negative feelings pass. Movies, concerts, and sporting events provide the opportunity to be caught up in the excitement of the crowd and carried along by our feelings for a little while. Enjoying music and attending sporting events certainly are not wrong. What is troublesome is when we expect these things to deliver the right feelings and thus to be a source of truth or authority.

I Think, Therefore . . .

Rationalism is knowledge or belief gained through reasoning. The fields of philosophy, science, and mathematics have long been the strongholds for rationalistic thought. This is mirrored in a perverse view of man's creativity and intellectual superiority in which such things are to be the source of truth and authority. Concepts that don't make sense to "the experts" are too easily and quickly rejected in today's culture, fostering the opinion, "I am right because I trust the experts on 'x.'" Educational credentials often become the sole basis for credibility. But educational credentials have their own agenda. Biblical teachings such as creation or miracles have been ruled out-of-bounds in much of academia.

Many questions from the disciplines of philosophy, science, and mathematics are designed to evoke a skeptical view of Christianity: "If there is a god, why are there not more positive miraculous occurrences and fewer calamities?"; "Why is there so much evil in the world if God is good?"; "Why would you put your trust in someone as narrow-minded as Jesus?" There are no philosophical, scientific, or mathematical formulae that can answer such questions. In a context of rationalism, this means that the questions themselves are designed to show the naiveté or irrelevance of religion. Raising the dead by a spoken word, rather than heroic, scientifically based medical means, is not an activity science has any real interest in affirming.

AUTHORITY'S AUTHOR

So how does the Christian respond to these challenges? How do we think about the empirical and the rational? How do we think about events recorded in the Bible when science disagrees? How do we think about the conflicts between Scripture and culture, or Scripture and philosophy, or Scripture and science, or . . . ? How do we face these difficulties and work through them in light of our Christian commitment and in light of God's Word?

If the tendency is to approach Scripture as inspirational reading, is it possible to view it as an absolute authority? To speak of the Bible's authority is to be perceived as being intolerant, which is seen as the mark of the simpleminded and unintelligent. Above all, today's generations seek to be open and teachable and loving. Jesus' words of exclusivity do not fit with the rational, reasoned voices calling for freedom in religious practice. It doesn't seem right or wise to speak openly about a religion that states there is only one way to God or that there is only one God. It just doesn't seem to make sense.

But doesn't the notion of "making sense" itself have its own cultural, philosophical, and scientific bias? Does it make sense that God would part a sea to allow an entire nation to walk through on dry ground? Does it make sense that out of all the stars and planets, our one solar system supports human life and is the recipient of his grace? Does it make sense that Jesus, who is divine, would take a human body and suffer physical pain? Does it make sense that God's incredible range of creativity in plants and flowers and animals was given for man's enjoyment? These things do not make sense to our rational or empirical processes. It is no wonder, then, that students ask why the Qur'an, the Book of Mormon, or the writings of Buddha or Confucius don't hold just as much authority as the Bible.

JESUS AND AUTHORITY

For the Christian, the question is, why should I stake my life and hope on the Christ of the Bible? Those who investigate the validity of Scientology, Christian Science, Ellen White and the Seventh Day Adventists, or groups like the Jehovah's Witnesses, have addressed the question of the authority of the Bible. The question is as old as history itself; it dates back to the garden of Eden and extends through the New Testament. An incident at the initiation of Jesus' public ministry will help us to focus the issue:

> Now when all the people were baptized, and when Jesus also had been baptized and was praying, the heavens were opened, and the Holy Spirit descended on him in bodily form, like a dove; and a voice came from heaven, "You are my beloved Son; with you I am well pleased." (Luke 3:21–22)

When Jesus Christ began his public ministry, he was declared by his heavenly Father to be his "beloved Son." This announcement did not escape the notice of the powers of darkness. Almost immediately after the Father announced his good pleasure in his Son, Jesus "was led by the Spirit in the wilderness for forty days, being tempted by the devil" (Luke 4:1–2).

How did the Devil begin his temptation? He wanted Jesus to give him proof that he was the Son of God. The question the Devil was asking was the question of truth and authority. He wanted to know how he could know that Jesus was God's only begotten Son. He wanted to know if it was true that Jesus was the Christ. So, he approached Jesus with three "opportunities"—three temptations through which Jesus could show the Devil, and show him conclusively, that he was the one the Father proclaimed him to be. The Devil gives Jesus three different offers. Two of the three are a demand for proof that Jesus was the Son of God, as the Father had said. Notice,

"*If you are the Son of God*, command this stone to become bread." (Luke 4:3)

And he took him to Jerusalem and set him on the pinnacle of the temple and said to him, "*If you are the Son of God*, throw yourself down from here." (Luke 4:9)

One way to think about this temptation in the wilderness is to see it as a challenge by Satan to Jesus. Satan demands that Jesus provide, to his satisfaction, the ground for truth and authority. The Devil was confronted with God himself, in his Son. But that was not enough; the Devil wanted proof, and so he demanded, "Show me."

In that light, it is important for us to ask: "How did Jesus respond to the Devil's requests?" How did Jesus "show" the Devil that he was who God the Father proclaimed him to be? Surely if Jesus is God he could have easily turned stones into bread. He could have thrown himself down from the pinnacle of the temple without harm. But he didn't.

Instead, Jesus turned the Devil's attention not to himself, but to God, and specifically to what God had said in his Word. In response to the challenge of authority, Jesus quoted Scripture. In response to the temptation to turn stones into bread, Jesus said, "It is written, 'Man shall not live by bread alone'" (Luke 4:4). Why did Jesus respond this way? The Devil wasn't asking about *how* we are to live or about whether one can live by bread alone. The Devil wanted Jesus to do something that no mere mortal could do. Did Jesus just dodge the challenge he was given? No, he didn't.

Jesus responds this way because he knows that the Devil's challenge will not be answered if Jesus performs some powerful act. The Devil's problem is not that he has failed to see God act in miraculous ways. The Devil's problem is the problem that plagues all who will not bow the knee to Christ; it is that he will not believe what God has said.

There was a similar temptation given many years before this one, as it turns out, by the same tempter. It was a temptation given not in the wilderness, but in a lush and plenteous garden:

> Now the serpent was more crafty than any other beast of the field that the LORD God had made.
>
> He said to the woman, "Did God actually say, 'You shall not eat of any tree in the garden'?" (Gen. 3:1)

The Devil does not come to Eve to tell her to disobey, at least not at first. He comes to Eve so that he might get her to question the word of God. And he tempts her by asking a question that is *close* to the truth, but is actually a denial of it. God had *not* said that Adam and Eve could not eat from any tree; he had said that there was one particular tree from which they were not to eat. The Devil knew that. His question was not one of curiosity. His question was designed to get Eve, and Adam after her, to disobey. And he succeeded.

When Jesus is tempted in the wilderness, he knows that the Devil's design is to get him to stop trusting what God has said. So, instead of arguing with the Devil about Jesus' own powers, Jesus replies to the Devil in a way that shows that he is trusting what God has said. Even though he has been in the wilderness for forty days, and even though he is hungry, he knows, *because God has said*, that his life is not defined by what he eats. It is defined by the "spiritual" food of God's Word. God had already said, "You are my beloved Son." No more proof was needed.

Here is Jesus, the perfect Son of God. If anyone could trust his own experience, it was Jesus. He could have been a perfect empiricist. If anyone could trust his own thinking, it was Jesus. He could have been a perfect rationalist. His experiences and his thinking were never affected by sin. They were perfect. But unlike us, though Jesus *could have* trusted himself, he didn't. He trusted God's Word alone.

Now, the question we must ask is, whom do you trust? Do you trust your own experience to guide you into all truth? Do you trust your own mind to give you all that is necessary for this life and the next? Or do you trust "every word that comes from the mouth of God" (Matt. 4:4)? Do you want to put your faith in yourself? Or would you rather put your faith in one in whom millions, for over two thousand years, have trusted, not only for their "spiritual food" in this life, but also in the life to come as well?

THE AUTHORITY OF THE SON

We have been discussing the problems unique to a "new" generation of people—people who have grown up in a context in which truth is supposed to be confined to each individual or group and in which the notion of authority, if applied at all, is meant to always be up for debate.

But, as we have been hinting all along, the problems that seem unique to this generation are not unique at all. Though contexts and concerns have varied over the centuries, the issues have not varied. They have remained relatively uniform throughout history.

Around two thousand years ago, there was a small but significant group of Hebrew Christians who were struggling with many of the same issues that we have been discussing.

The contexts, of course, were different. We should not expect that the issues faced by first-century Hebrew Christians would conform exactly to those faced by twenty-first-century folk. Though the contexts in which the Hebrews struggled and lived were different, the contours of their struggle were, at significant points, coincident with ours.

One of the occasions for writing the epistle to the Hebrews was that issues of truth and authority—issues that this group of Jewish Christians had, in the past, addressed by its strong commitment to Christ—were now under suspicion.

The Jewish people had a rich and deep tradition. It was a tradition that has no equal in history. As we write this, the United States has just celebrated another July 4. That date is set aside to mark the beginning of a new nation, now well over 200 years old. Though that may seem like a long history, it is merely a blink compared to the history of Israel.

God treated Israel unlike any other nation on the face of the earth, working mightily and miraculously for their sake. In the

United States, debates have swirled around the question as to whether God was "on our side" in various conflicts and wars. But there was no need for such debates in Israel. God had declared to Israel that he was on their side (see Gen. 17:8; Jer. 24:7; 31:33; 32:38; Ezek. 11:20; 37:23, 27; Zech. 8:8).

But, as is often the case, Israel's strength became her weakness. One of the things that plagued the Hebrew community to which this epistle was written was that it was in danger of letting its rich and deep traditions eclipse the truth.

Throughout history, the people of God had lived out their relationship to God by way of relying on God's appointed messengers. In some instances, those messengers were angels (see Gen. 19:1–22; 28:12; Ps. 91:11). In others, the chosen messenger of the Lord was Moses (see the book of Exodus). In still others, Israel was to live out its relationship to God according to the appointed Levitical priesthood (see Deut. 17:9, 18; 18:1; 24:8; 27:9; Josh. 3:3; 8:33; 2 Chron. 5:5, 12; 23:18; Jer. 33:18, 21–26; Ezek. 43:19; 44:15; Heb. 7:11).

To rely on these messengers, *as God's appointed messengers*, was not sinful; indeed, a lack of trust in these messengers would have been tantamount to a lack of trust in God. God had appointed them for various tasks, at various times in history. As appointed by God to serve him, they were also meant to be trusted with the tasks God had given them.

Part of the problem that the author to the Hebrews had to address was the confusion that had set in since Jesus Christ had come. Those messengers that were at one time and place the chosen vehicles for God's purposes for his people had now been, once and for all time, replaced by Christ himself.

Yet some were still tempted to put their confidence in lesser things—things that were, in themselves, not sinful, but were nevertheless not meant to be the "focus or locus" of their confidence and trust. These Christians had mistaken the *instrument* through which God's truth and authority came with that truth and authority itself.

And now we can begin to see that the problems immediately addressed in the book of Hebrews are problems that relate to our twenty-first-century predicaments. We should expect no less, since God has seen fit to give us, in his Word, principles that are applicable across the historical spectrum. We will look at these principles in the opening verses of this epistle:

> Long ago, at many times and in many ways, God spoke to our fathers by the prophets, but in these last days he has spoken to us by his Son, whom he appointed the heir of all things, through whom also he created the world. He is the radiance of the glory of God and the exact imprint of his nature, and he upholds the universe by the word of his power. After making purification for sins, he sat down at the right hand of the Majesty on high, having become as much superior to angels as the name he has inherited is more excellent than theirs. (Heb. 1:1–4)

Notice how abruptly the author begins this epistle. Compared to so many other epistles in Scripture, where Paul, for example, will first introduce himself, this epistle stands out as unique. It is so unique that many surmise that this letter was a sermon preached and then written to these Jewish Christians.

There were serious problems in this community of Christian Hebrews. The people were in danger of drifting away from the faith and of neglecting the salvation that had come to them (2:1–3); their disobedience was about to get the best of them, even as it had their forefathers in the wilderness (chapter 4); they were immature, not because they were recent converts (by this time, they should have been teachers), but because they had become dull of hearing (5:11–12). They still needed spiritual milk and were not prepared for solid food. So serious was their immaturity that some were in danger of irretrievably losing the salvation they had previously claimed to have (6:1–20). So, the author writes this word of encouragement (13:22) to bring about repentance unto life.

It should strike us, therefore, that the author begins not with a personal introduction or even with a direct response to these serious problems, but with an acknowledgment of the rich and deep tradition of God's dealings with his people.

We should not pass over the first verse too quickly. The author is quick to point out that *God* indeed spoke to his people in various ways and at different times. The Hebrew Christians who received this epistle had not been wrong about their own tradition (at least not initially). They were right to see God's use of angels, and of Moses, and of the Levitical priests as important aspects of his relationship to them. The problem was not with the *instruments* of God's revelation through history. The problem was that some among them now wanted those instruments to become the ultimate *source* and *ground* of truth and authority for them. They had misplaced their notion of truth and of authority. Sound familiar?

We discussed the two primary sources of authority and truth that are often put forth: the senses (empiricism) and the mind (rationalism). These are not sources that have been chosen by God as messengers of his special revelation. But we, like this group of Hebrews, have mistaken these good and necessary *instruments* for ultimate sources or grounds of truth.

The question of authority is one that, perhaps now more than in times past, occupies center stage in much of contemporary discussion. Whatever postmodernism's identity, one of its abiding tenets was first set forth by Jean-François Lyotard and is contained in his (in)famous phrase that the postmodern condition is marked by an "incredulity toward metanarratives." This phrase is not as opaque as it may at first seem. Lyotard's point was simply that there should be no overarching and overriding principle or system (a metanarrative) that would determine the shape and direction of what we claim to know and believe. To put it another way, we are to reject such universal principles or systems. This has the effect of destroying any principle or system that would unify otherwise disparate beliefs or "truths." It also has the effect of assuring us that there is no universal authoritative principle or system that applies to our own set of beliefs and practices.

Under the influence of this tenet, the question of truth and authority becomes paramount. I may decide that truth for me is whatever I can practice without causing personal harmful consequences. If I can sit at my computer and access illegal material without harming anyone, then it must be that such material is "true" for me; it is a legitimate understanding of "reality" for me. There can be no constraints against my actions; no authority that can hinder them. If I can engage in relationships that are personally satisfying to all involved, then such relationships must be "true" for us all. To paraphrase one postmodern, "Truth is whatever I can get away with." It is simply a matter of personal taste based on personal preference and practice.

Whatever it was that plagued these Hebrews, the author wants to make sure that his readers get the truth and authority matter settled before anything else can be addressed (and there is much more, as we will see, that *needs* to be addressed). The same is true for us (and for this book). Unless we settle the matter of authority first, we will be forever confused and confounded with the issues that press in on us every day. We may be able to live with the decisions we make on a daily basis; we may even be able to find others who are living with the same confusion. But "living with" such decisions and beliefs is only a way of avoiding what we know to be true. It is only a thin shield, able to mask and cover the reality that is deep within us.

What is it, then, that we need to know about God's authority and truth? What is it that will solidify us, that will plant us firmly, so that we will not be confused and tossed about by every new idea that comes to us? It is the same thing that these Hebrews needed to know. It is that, though God chose various means of revealing himself to his people throughout history, all of those means were simply channels, rivers, and tributaries of God's revelation, flowing toward and leading inexorably to that great ocean of final revelation that God has given to us in his Son.

This is the first point to understand. God has spoken in Christ. Or, as the author of Hebrews puts it more pointedly, God has spoken (literally) "in a Son." The reason that the author writes this way ("in *a* Son" rather than "in *the* Son") is not to highlight that Christ is a son among many sons. Given everything else that the author says about Christ in these few verses, the point he is making is a categorical one. In past times, God did speak through appointed means—"*by* prophets." But now, God has revealed himself by means of a completely different category of revelation; now he is revealed "by Son."

The Hebrews would have seen the tremendous import of this categorical shift. It was a shift that was declaring those former means of revelation to be past their time of usefulness. It was a shift from using human and temporary means of revelation to God now using himself as the final mode of revelation to his people.

Note also how the author frames the temporal categories. This revelation, "by Son," is the completion of a long history of God's revelation to his people. As completing God's revelation, the Son is in continuity with what God had done in the past, but is also uniquely discontinuous with what God had done previously. God spoke "long ago" or (as it could also be translated) "for a long time" at various times and in various ways "by the prophets." Here the author acknowledges the history of God's revelation to his people.

It is worth noticing in this opening chapter of Hebrews just how the author chooses to cite Old Testament references. Even though he quotes from Deuteronomy, 2 Samuel, and the Psalms, he is not concerned to note the human instruments God used to write these works. Rather, he notes in every case that this is what *God* says (1:5–13). In each case, the author states that God said these things. This is *God speaking* (through different human instruments) "long ago" at various times and in various ways. He then connects that history with the revelation that has come in the Son. This is its continuity.

More significant, however, is the way in which the author highlights the radical *discontinuity* between this diverse way of God revealing himself and the now climactic revelation that has come in Christ. The revelation that has come in the Son has come "in these last days." But just exactly why are these days "the last"?

The answer to that question points us again to God's revelation. The reason these days are the *last* days, is because God's *last* revelation has been given. The "days" of God's calendar are, in other words, defined not first of all by their length or their number on a calendar. The days of God are defined by the *kind* or *category* of revelation that he gives at a particular time in history.

To put the matter another way, if these days were not the last, then there would necessarily be another, and more, revelation that God would give in history. Not only so, but the clear implication would be, from what the author says, that the revelation given "in a Son" was itself insufficient and incomplete; more, better, and clearer revelation would still be needed.

But the logic of the author's argument in these first few, magnificently rich verses is striking in its opposition to such an idea. This Son, in whom God has now lastly spoken, is "the radiance of the glory of God and the exact imprint of his nature." It would be difficult to find a more exalted description of Christ. The two phrases, "the radiance of the glory of God" and "the exact imprint of his nature," are meant to say virtually the same thing in two different ways.

Students of the Bible will readily recognize echoes of the beginning of the gospel of John in our passage. This should not be surprising, since, in spite of the different contexts and concerns of the author to the Hebrews and the apostle John, God authored both books. So, after John clearly sets forth the fact that the second person of the Trinity, the Word, is himself God (John 1:1), lest there be any mistake, he asserts, "And the Word became flesh and dwelt among us, and we have seen his glory, glory as of the only Son from the Father, full of grace and truth" (John 1:14).

This Word, who is God, came down to dwell among us. And this One who came was not only the Word, he was the Son. John then recalls the time when he, with Peter and James, was given the opportunity, on the mountain, to see this Son in his eternal glory (Matt. 17:1–13, Mark 9:2–8). He recounts this event in the context of his declaration that the Word dwelt among us to emphasize that the dwelling with us in no way eliminated the great truth that this Word was God. His glory was "as of the only Son from the Father." The glory that John saw was "the radiance of the glory of God." It pointed to the fact that this Word, this Son, remained, even as he dwelt among us, "the exact imprint" of God's very nature.

These Hebrew Christians would have understood that the glory of which the author spoke was the very glory of God—his *shekinah* presence with his people (see Ex. 24:15–18) that was now revealed in the Son.

Is it any wonder, then, that the revelation that has now been given in the Son is the final and completed revelation from God? If that revelation was not only "in the Son" but was, in fact, *God himself* revealing himself, is it even possible that there might be more, better, or clearer revelation to come in history? How could there be an expectation of "more" or "better" when the highest and exalted One *himself* has condescended to reveal himself to us? Wouldn't any other revelation pale in comparison to the revelation that we have in the very Son of God himself, especially since this Son is the radiance of Yahweh's glory and the exact imprint of his nature?

But notice that the author of Hebrews is not only concerned that we understand clearly who this Son is. That is crucial. But it is just as crucial that we understand not only that the revelation that has come to us in the Son has come simply and only in his *person*, but also (and this is all-important for our purposes) that *God has spoken to us* in this Son. The author is not concerned simply with Christ as *personal* revelation, but he is primarily concerned (in this passage) to emphasize that God *has spoken* to us in this one who is "true God of true God."

In other words, it is the Person of the Word of God as he gives to his church the *written* Word of God that is paramount in the author's mind. The point his readers need to see, as do we, is that *God has spoken* through this final and complete revelation of himself in his Son.

This Son, through whom God has finally and lastly spoken, is the one who, having made purification of sins, "sat down at the right hand of the Majesty on high." There is no more exalted view of the *authority* of God to a Hebrew mind than this. To sit at God's right hand is to have all the authority of God himself. It is to *be* God himself in his sovereign capacity to reign (Pss. 60:5; 63:8; Matt. 26:64; Acts 2:33–34; 7:55; Rom. 8:34; Eph. 1:20; Col. 3:1; Rev. 5:1, 7). So important is this to the author that he places the thought at strategic places in his letter (see Heb. 1:3, 13; 8:1; 10:12; 12:2). He wants his readers to understand that this Son who has spoken has been given all authority in heaven and on earth (Matt. 28:18).

The "truth" question and the "authority" question are all summed up in the Person. That much is clear. But for the church in "these last days," the issues of truth and authority are summed up in the written *Word* of the Son in Holy Scripture. The truth of God and the authority of God are summed up in what God has spoken in his Son.

HAS GOD SAID?

But questions linger—questions that relate specifically to our current predicament. If *God* has spoken, how can we know such a thing? Don't we need the foundation of our senses, or our mental faculties, or both, to *know* that God has spoken? And if our senses and mental faculties are subject to so many variables, how can they be trusted to give us anything but probability?

In Charles Dickens' classic tale, *A Christmas Carol*, Ebenezer Scrooge meets the spirit of his old business partner, Jacob Marley, for the first time, seven years after Marley's death. But Scrooge is initially skeptical:

> "You don't believe in me," observed the Ghost.
>
> "I don't," said Scrooge.
>
> "What evidence would you have of my reality, beyond that of your senses?"
>
> "I don't know," said Scrooge.

"Why do you doubt your senses?"

"Because," said Scrooge, "a little thing affects them. A slight disorder of the stomach makes them cheats. You may be an undigested bit of beef, a blot of mustard, a crumb of cheese, a fragment of an underdone potato. There's more of gravy than of grave about you, whatever you are!"[2]

We all know that our senses and our mental faculties, no matter how acute, are too feeble and fickle to be ultimately trustworthy as *sources* of truth. This does *not* mean that they are not *instruments* of truth, but they are not equipped to generate what is needed when the source or ground of truth and authority is in question. Not only so, but since the entrance of sin in the world, we have a sinful bent against ultimate truth and authority, unless God so changes our hearts as to rejoice in such things.

So what can provide what we need? Is there any way to be sure that God's Word is just that—*his* Word? These questions seem to dominate our times, when all authority and certainty are being questioned. They are important questions; they are questions that get at the root of our relationship to God. In order to address these typical and natural questions, we need to delve more deeply into what we mean when we speak of the "ground" of truth and authority.

The question of the ground or foundation of the world and everything in it is not a new one.[3] As far back (at least) as the philosopher Aristotle, the question of the ground of everything else was discussed and debated. In such debates, two things were

2. Charles Dickens, *A Christmas Carol* (London: Chapman & Hall, 1845), 27.

3. We will use the term *ground* here as a kind of technical term and for simplicity's sake. Historically, however, the term used in theology was *principia*, which is translated as "foundations" or "sources." It is a term that has its roots in the Greek term *archē*, which means a beginning point, a source, or a first principle.

clear: (1) whatever ground we determine to be in place, it must be such that it has nothing behind or beyond it. To posit something behind or beyond this ground would make that thing the ground; (2) it is impossible to continue positing a ground, of a ground, of a ground, of a ground, etc. For a ground to be a ground it has to be that upon which everything else rests. Aristotle argued that all grounds or first principles or beginning points are the "first point from which a thing either is or comes to be or is known." In other words, "grounds," according to Aristotle, provide the bedrock foundation for everything that is or is known. This concept of a beginning point, what some have called an Archimedean point, is a necessary and crucial aspect of everything that we think, indeed, of everything that *is*.[4] Aristotle understood this, philosophy has continued to articulate this idea, and Christian theology has seen it as basic to its own discipline.

We can think of grounds, by analogy, the way we think of the physical ground underneath us. What is it that supports the room that I am now in? It is the boards in the floor. But what supports those boards? The beams underneath. What supports those beams? It is the ground underneath and around those beams. What supports the ground? Well, the ground supports itself. It is the support without which nothing else could be a support. As is the case physically, so it is with questions of ultimate authority, truth, etc. There is a "place" beyond which we cannot go and without which we cannot move. That place is the ground or "grounds."

The theology that was resurrected during the time of the Reformation (sixteenth century) and beyond argued that all disciplines, especially theology, require grounds, and that such

4. Because it was Archimedes who said, "Give me a place to stand and I will move the world."

grounds partake of at least the following characteristics: (1) they are necessarily and unchangeably true, and (2) they must be known *per se*, that is, in themselves, as both immediate and indemonstrable. "Immediate" here means that the status of a ground is not taken from something external to it, but is inherent in the thing itself. It does not mean, strictly speaking, that nothing mediates the truth therein, but rather that nothing external to the ground mediates that truth. Similarly, "indemonstrable" here means that the fact of a ground is not proven by way of argument using principles external to that ground, but is such that it provides the ground upon which any other fact or demonstration depends.

This concern for grounds, historically, had its focus in two primary disciplines: philosophy and theology. In philosophy, the concern was expressed in the thought and philosophy of René Descartes. For all that separated Descartes's philosophy from the Protestant theology of his day—and there was much that did—the concern for grounds was common to both. Descartes thought that his grounds were "clear and distinct ideas" concerning first the self and then God. These two, in that order, were supposed to provide the foundation for everything else that could be known. But Descartes' rationalism (since he wanted to begin with innate *ideas*) only led to skepticism.

Christian theologians during this time argued, against rationalism, that grounds could never be located in the human self. To do so would lead to the kind of skepticism that followed in the wake of Descartes' philosophy. What, then, is the ground of theology? What is it that can provide the foundation, the source and beginning point of all truth and authority? To ask the question is almost to answer it.

In the Westminster Confession of Faith (perhaps the ablest expression of Protestant doctrine in the entire history of the church), the authors set out, for the first time in church history, a *Protestant* doctrine of Scripture. In chapter 1 of the Confession, section 4, the authors wrote:

> The authority of the Holy Scripture, for which it ought to be believed, and obeyed, dependeth not upon the testimony of any man, or Church; but wholly upon God (who is truth itself) the author thereof: and therefore it is to be received, because it is the Word of God.

Notice that the subject of this section is the *authority* of Scripture. They are answering the question of *grounds* for such authority. On what *grounds* does this authority depend?

It does not depend on any man or church. This was stated, negatively, to make clear that this was a Protestant and not a Roman Catholic doctrine of Scripture. But notice here that the authors say, in effect, that the authority of Holy Scripture depends on its *author*. It is the *author* of Holy Scripture who makes Scripture what it is.

The fact of the matter is, if we fail to see Holy Scripture as authored by God, and therefore as the *ground* of its own authority, we will fail to understand what Scripture actually is.

And, as the Confession makes clear, if we want to know why we should accept Holy Scripture as the Word of God, it is "*because it is the Word of God.*" That is, not *simply* because it says that it is; many books make such claims. Rather, we accept it because God is its author and *God* says that it is. To appeal to something behind, above, or beyond this is to think of Scripture (and God) as something other than the ground of truth and authority.

Isn't this what Jesus himself was saying to the Devil in the wilderness? Jesus had the power to show Satan who he was. But

40

Jesus also knew that whatever he did would detract from Satan's central objection. His objection was not that he hadn't seen all he needed to see. Jesus knew that Satan's objection was focused on the fact that he did not believe what God had said.

Jesus illustrated this same principle in the parable of the rich man and Lazarus (Luke 16:19–31). The rich man in Hades asks that there be demonstrations of power and miracles displayed to his five brothers so that they might not suffer the same torment. What is the response to this request? "If they do not hear Moses and the Prophets, neither will they be convinced if someone should rise from the dead" (Luke 16:31).

Hearing "Moses and the Prophets" means hearing the Word of God. Jesus reminds the rich man that his brothers, like him, have all that is needed to avoid the torment of Hades. They have the Word of God that was spoken "by the prophets" and by Moses, and that has now been spoken "in the Son."

John 6:60–71 gives us the same truth. There Jesus is teaching many of his disciples that the only way one may come to him is if the Father grants it. The message must have gotten through; it was a message that stripped away any hope of salvation by human merit or action. That message has never been a popular one. So, in the course of Jesus' instruction, "many of his disciples turned back and no longer walked with him" (6:66).

Jesus then asked the twelve if they, too, would turn away. Simon Peter's answer is instructive: "Lord, to whom shall we go? You have the words of eternal life" (6:68).

Peter's question gets to the heart of the matter as we think about the ground of authority and truth. Where else can we go but to the word of Christ himself? He alone has the words of eternal life. Is there any other standard, principle, or foundation that carries with it the authority of God himself? Is there any other standard, principle, or foundation that just *is* God himself, revealed in the flesh and thus giving to us "the words of eternal life"?

A FIRM FOUNDATION

In the hymn "How Firm a Foundation," the author begins by attesting to the fact that the foundation that we have in the Word of God is both firm and complete:

> How firm a foundation, ye saints of the Lord, is laid for your
> faith in his excellent word!
> What more can he say than to you he hath said, to you who
> for refuge to Jesus have fled?

The foundation that we have in God's Holy Word is firm. It is secure. It is certain. It is the ground upon which anything else—any truth or any authority—must rest. And the question asked in this stanza is meant to be rhetorical: What more *can* he say? God has spoken through his own Son. No other revelation can compare; no other revelation is needed.

And so, we can now see why the Word of God cannot be broken. It has its roots in God speaking through his various agents in history. It has its climax in God speaking through his Son. It has its focus in God speaking in every word of Holy Scripture, which is, itself, God's own speech.

No wonder Newton, as he contemplated this great truth, asked, "On the Rock of Ages founded, what can shake thy sure repose?" No wonder this truth gave him confidence in those things "that cannot be shaken" (Heb. 12:28). What, indeed, can shake thy sure repose? The Word of God, and the salvation it offers, are founded on the Rock of Ages.

No current trends, no sophisticated arguments, no intense

temptation has the power to break that Rock. If it is on Christ the solid rock we stand, then we are always and everywhere protected from such onslaughts in the shadow of his mighty wings.

With salvation's walls surrounded,
Thou may'st smile at all thy foes.

DISCUSSION QUESTIONS

1. What is the average person's general idea of authority?
2. Is there anything in your life that you use as an escape or avoidance? How can distraction be a means of escape? What are some examples in your own life?
3. "Some may base their lives on what they feel like doing at any given time." How often do we not do something based on not "feeling" like doing it? Do we sometimes rely too heavily on our emotions?
4. In the wilderness, Satan tries to tempt Jesus, but Jesus redirects the temptation and points back to God. In what ways does Jesus accomplish this? How may we use this method in our lives?
5. As you examine your heart, do you find ways in which you, like the Israelites, are tempted to idolize the messengers of the Bible rather than focusing on God? Explain.
6. What are two sources of authority that are often misused? Are they ultimate grounds of truth?
7. What are the reasons the Word of God cannot be broken?
8. What is the final revelation that God has given us? How can God now categorize this as his last revelation?

2: OUR DEEPEST NEED

SEE! THE STREAMS OF LIVING WATERS

See! the streams of living waters
Springing from eternal love,
Well supply thy sons and daughters,
And all fear of want remove:
Who can faint, while such a river
Ever flows their thirst t'assuage?
Grace, which, like the Lord, the giver,
Never fails from age to age.

The Word of God is our ground, our foundation. It is the place upon which we stand, because it is Christ alone who has the words of eternal life.

But it is not enough simply to acknowledge this truth. It is a first step, but it will have no effect in our lives unless we apply that truth to our own thinking and living. We have to "own" the truth of God's Word if we honestly claim to believe it. It is possible, as James reminds us, to have beliefs that we do not own, beliefs that make no difference in our obedience to God (see James 2:18–19). Having settled the truth and authority question, we will now begin to think about how we might make application of that truth and authority in our own lives.

LOST AT SEA?

We have all likely known people who have said, "I need some time away to try to find myself." Perhaps we have friends who are tirelessly trying to figure out who they are. These inward journeys and explorations raise a basic question: Why is it that we don't know who we are as we live our lives in the context of the here and now? A natural follow-up question is, how do we figure out who we are?

These questions are not peculiar to this postmodern era. Since the fall of man, people have struggled both on the horizontal (or relational) level and at the "self" level to try to find themselves. Both of these struggles take us all the way back to the garden. There we find out that we are lost, because in our sins we hope not to be found.

After Adam ate the forbidden fruit (Genesis 3), he attempted to hide—naked and ashamed. God asked Adam, "Where are you?" This question does not point to a deficiency in God's omniscience. It is not that God did not know Adam's and Eve's physical location. The question was not framed for the purpose of providing information for God. The question goes to Adam's heart and to the heart of every man and woman on earth.

Like all of us, Adam and Eve were graciously placed in God's creation. They were responsible, under God, to live and work in God's world according to God's own design (see Gen. 1:28–29; 2:15–17, 19–20, 24). But Adam and Eve sinned against God, and their reaction to that sin was to attempt to hide from God (Gen. 3:8). When God came to have fellowship with them, they were hiding. And so he asked, "Where are you?" It was a question designed to highlight that even though they were still living in God's world, they were no longer "with" God. The fellowship that God had established between himself and them had been broken. Instead of being with God, they were hoping to be separate from him.

Neither is God's question, "Where are you?" a question of location. It is a question that points to our relationship to God. In that sense, the question, "Where are you?" is identical to the question, "Who are you?" With respect to our relationship to God, the answer to one is the answer to the other.

For centuries, expositors of the Bible have stressed the importance of the vertical, or God-to-man, relationship as the necessary basis for understanding who and where we are. Philosophers and theologians alike have often encouraged people to think about where and who they are in relation to God. In the fourth century, Augustine of Hippo confessed that because God created us for his own glory, our hearts remain restless until we find our rest in him. In the opening sentence of John Calvin's *Institutes*, Calvin insightfully sets out the radical truth that true knowledge of ourselves depends first on a true knowledge of God. The mathematician and theologian Pascal wrote about the "God-shaped emptiness" within human beings. God created us to know him, to be able to stand before him naked and unashamed as Adam and Eve did before the fall. Our need to know who we are, and who he is, is a need embedded in us since creation. It cannot be excised from the created heart of man.

How, then, should we think about this need? Are there categories that can help us understand just how to think about our indelible need to know God truly and, in knowing him, to truly know ourselves?

SKIMMING THE SURFACE: FELT NEEDS

There are doubtless better categories to use, but suppose for convenience we think about our predicament in terms of "felt" and "unfelt" needs. The predicament itself, we should note, is brought about because of the fall into sin. Prior to the fall, our need to be in relationship to God was met so completely that no distinction between felt and unfelt needs was present. But sin has changed all that.

Consider Adam and Eve just after the fall. Their felt needs and unfelt needs became radically confused and conflicted. They were naked, but now ashamed. The nakedness that was natural before they had sinned became an embarrassment to them now that sin was in their hearts and in the world. They perceived, rightly, that they needed to be covered. In that perception, however, they also perceived that they could "cover" themselves from God and his presence. This latter perception was grossly inaccurate; it was nothing more than self-deception. The last thing that they needed was to be removed from God's presence. Even given their sin, they were still creatures of God, created and sustained by him at every moment. To be removed from him would be, ultimately, to cease to "be." Instead of seeing their now even more desperate need for God, they thought it best to be removed from him altogether.

Because of sin, we are no different from Adam and Eve hiding in the garden. Like them, we all are created in God's image. Because we are images of God, we cannot be removed from him without at the same time ceasing to "be." Yet, if we act according to our sins, we try to hide from him; we think it best to try to remove him from us. The tragedy of this self-deception is that in thinking we can eradicate God from our thoughts and lives, we engage in the attempted eradication of our true selves.

Modern descriptions of psychological and emotional struggles do not provide categories that acknowledge our attempts to hide from God. We may be correct in our diagnosis of felt needs when we describe ourselves, for example, as lonely or confused. But since the fall, there are deeper needs that we have which remain un- or misdiagnosed. The essential human components of mind, emotion, and will were deadened by the fall. Therefore, if we remain in our sins and apart from Christ, it is impossible for us to think correctly—about God or about ourselves.

We set our affections on the wrong things in an effort to enhance our lives with fulfilling relationships and enjoyable things and circumstances. Pleasing self, in an effort to find peace and happiness, is both the default mode of the human condition (after the fall) as well as its driving, conscious force. In seeking to meet our felt needs, all the while ignoring or misdiagnosing our unfelt needs, we inevitably turn to perverse and damaging solutions.

According to those who work on college campuses (administrators, faculty, and campus ministers), there are many bizarre behaviors and addictions among students, some of which are literally destroying their lives. In many cases, intensive counseling will reveal selfish needs at the root of these ugly and destructive practices.

Counselors report that a student's perceived need for power and control is often expressed in eating disorders. Some have said that the need to be accepted by one's peers can be demonstrated by drinking to excess. Promiscuity as a cure for loneliness is seen in the upsurge of all kinds of sexual perversions and sex without commitment. Unfortunately, some polls indicate that these sins are as common among Christians as they are among non-Christians. Why are young, healthy adults, full of promise and potential, bent on apparent self-destruction?

An even more troubling, and telling, form of perverse behavior is the more recent but sadly all-too-common trend toward cutting and self-injury:[1]

1. According to an Associated Press article, nearly one in five students who completed a mental-health survey at two Ivy League colleges said they deliberately injured themselves as a way to relieve stress or cry out for emotional help. See "Nearly 1 in 5

Kevin sits alone in his dark dorm room on a Tuesday night. To his professors and friends, this 20 year-old college sophomore is a "regular guy." But tonight, Kevin's academic and relational pressures combine with ongoing family difficulties in a mix that leaves him feeling angry and out of control. He's not crazy. He's not suicidal. But something is definitely wrong.

Kevin responds to his roller-coaster emotional state through a distressing and regular ritual that's become his secret coping mechanism. He removes his shirt and runs a razor blade across his stomach and chest. When finished, he's covered with a mess of bleeding cuts. Amazingly, he says he "feels better."[2]

The same article recounts the story of a young woman who engaged in the practice of cutting:

During my late childhood and adolescence I experienced prolonged emotional stress. My parents went through a messy divorce, using us kids as pawns to hurt each other. I was sexually abused. My mother died. My best friend died . . . for me, (these events) were overwhelming. At the age of 13, I found that self-injury temporarily relieved the unbearable jumble of feelings. I cut myself in the bathroom, where razor blades were handy and I could lock the door. The slicing through flesh never hurt . . . it never even occurred to me that it should . . . the blood brought an odd sense of well-being, or strength . . . sometimes I rubbed the blood on my face and arms and looked at myself in the mirror. I did not think how sick I must be.

Students at 2 Ivy League Schools Practice Self-Abuse," *Associated Press*, June 5, 2006, http://www.foxnews.com/story/2006/06/05/study-nearly-1-in-5-students-at-2-ivy-league-schools-practice-self-abuse.html.

2. Walt Mueller, "Crying through Their Cuts," accessed April 7, 2016, http://www.cpyu.org/resource/crying-through-their-cuts.

I did not think. With a safe sense of detachment, I watched myself play with my own flowing blood. The fireball of tension was gone and I was calm. I learned to soothe myself this way.[3]

Obviously, there is a need inside both Kevin and this young woman that even they have yet to grasp. Their behavior initially seems strangely beneficial, but then later does not make sense to them. How could the purposeful infliction of physical pain bring pleasure? Why such confusion? Why resort to habits of self-destruction?

Some of these sins, such as sex, drinking, or pornography, may have their own perverse rationale; they may seem to make sense to some of us; they may provide some temporary enjoyment. They are considered pleasurable, self-indulgent activities, even if their aftermath may cause negative consequences, especially when considered from the perspective of eternity. But, deep down, we all know (though we wish we could erase that knowledge) that such behavior only masks what lies beneath.

THE UNDERCURRENT OF UNFELT NEEDS

Just what is it that lies beneath? What is behind the need for personal gratification, even if it causes intense physical or emotional pain? Why do we perceive a need for control, power, and acceptance? Why are there relational breakdowns? What causes these perceived feelings of emptiness? What can fill the craving, and why is it so difficult to satisfy? Behind all the felt needs, there seems to be one primary, unfelt need. There is a spiritual DNA in the makeup of human beings that they are unable to map on their own.

3. Ibid.

The apostle Paul, in the first chapter of the epistle to the Romans, under the inspiration of the Holy Spirit, probes deeply into this psychological state. He is concerned to show that all people, as created in God's image, are unable to remove the constant "voice" of God from their own consciences. In the deep recesses of the human heart the question from Eden echoes: "Where are you?" Hence the quest, the exploration, the journey into self.

Notice how Paul explains our psychological makeup now that sin has perverted our conscience:

> For the wrath of God is revealed from heaven against all ungodliness and unrighteousness of men, who by their unrighteousness suppress the truth. For what can be known about God is plain to them, because God has shown it to them. For his invisible attributes, namely, his eternal power and divine nature, have been clearly perceived, ever since the creation of the world, in the things that have been made. So they are without excuse. (Rom. 1:18–20)

Paul is explaining what it means for us to be the image of God, but without Christ, still in our sins. Part of what it means is that the wrath of God abides on us. But it also means that there is a process, almost mechanistic, that serves to trigger this wrath from God. It is a process of self-deception. We claim not to know something we inevitably cannot escape. We convince ourselves that we are ignorant, when as a matter of fact, we know we are not.

To put it in terms of Genesis 3, knowing God, we attempt to hide from him, even as Adam and Eve did. We perceive God in all that is made, including *ourselves*, but we think it best to run from him. We will not have him in our thoughts or in our lives. Paul continues:

For although they knew God, they did not honor him as God or give thanks to him, but they became futile in their thinking, and their foolish hearts were darkened. Claiming to be wise, they became fools, and exchanged the glory of the immortal God for images resembling mortal man and birds and animals and creeping things. (Rom. 1:21–23)

Yes, Paul is clear that we know God. But the sin that dominates our hearts (if we are not in Christ) is determined to take that knowledge and hold it down as much as possible. This process moves us to foolishness, to darkened hearts, to a perverse and irrational exchange. We exchange the truth that we know, the truth God gives us of who he is, for images of created things. In other words, sin moves us from a knowledge of God to a self-deceptive denial of that knowledge.

But this denial is nothing abstract. Paul is not concerned here simply with what we claim to know or not to know. Rather, the denial of the knowledge of God moves us to act in certain ways. In this perverse exchange, those activities and actions that should be the result of knowing God—activities such as wisdom and worship—become twisted and perverted. Instead of wisdom (which is the application of true knowledge), we engage in foolishness (which is the application of wrong beliefs). We create idols for ourselves. We even trust that these idols will give us what only God can give us—true pleasure and satisfaction.

Paul's language gets even stronger:

They exchanged the truth about God for a lie and worshiped and served the creature rather than the Creator, who is blessed forever! Amen. (Rom. 1:25)

Notice carefully what Paul says here. In the exchange of the truth about God for a lie, we wind up with . . . *worship*. This may seem to be a strange way to describe something perverse and unseemly. We are used to associating the notion of worship with religion and with commitment. But that is exactly Paul's point! As images of God we never avoid the activity of worship. The question to be asked is not *whether* we worship but *what* or *whom*.

This goes a long way toward explaining the otherwise enigmatic and mysterious behavior that we noticed above. When we, with Paul, view such behavior in the context of worship, we are better able to see certain bizarre behavior for what it is. For example, why would someone be so devoted to sexual perversion, or alcohol, or self-mutilation, even in the face of the destruction that such practices bring about?

Paul's answer to the question is simple. We must worship something. And if our misdiagnosis of our felt needs leads us to pursue something created rather than the Creator, then we will attach ourselves to that created thing *religiously*. We will, in fact, worship it; we will give our very lives, sometimes literally, for it.

Our unfelt need is, therefore, something quite familiar to us. It is something we know but suppress. It is like an undercurrent at sea—always there, strong and persistent, but hidden behind the surface "calm" of the visible water. It is the knowledge of God our Creator who "gives to all mankind life and breath and everything" (Acts 17:25). But the need remains unfelt because we suppress it, not because we are ignorant of it. The only way to bring this unfelt need to the surface, as we will see shortly, is in the good news of the gospel of Jesus Christ.

BROKEN CISTERNS

The apostle John, in his gospel (chapter 4), tells the story of a Samaritan woman's encounter with Jesus. Jesus brought

her face to face with her felt needs, the needs that had driven
her to seek satisfaction in intimate relationships with at least
six different men. Jesus was sitting by Jacob's well, resting after
traveling from Judea. It was the middle of the day. A woman of
Samaria approached the well, and Jesus asked her for a drink. She
was taken aback by his request, and for two very good reasons.
One, Jesus was a Jew. This was probably obvious to the woman
by his dress and speech. She was a Samaritan. Jewish people,
by the woman's own assertion, had "no dealings with Samari-
tans." She would have been surprised at both Jesus' willingness
to communicate with her and his willingness to drink from a
Samaritan well. Second, she would also have been surprised at
his speaking with a woman in public, particularly a Samaritan
woman. His disciples "marveled" that he was talking to a woman
at all (v. 27).

Jesus had purposefully passed through Samaria after leaving
Judea to return to Galilee. Since he was and is all knowing, he
planned this encounter at the well. As John makes clear, Jesus
knew about this woman's life and her emptiness. Her five husbands had not satisfied her. As Jesus meets her, she was trying
again to find fulfillment with a sixth man who was not her husband. She was looking for satisfaction and love, but her solutions
were all wrong; they only drove her to try more wrong solutions.

She was actively, consciously seeking to fulfill the desires of
her heart on the horizontal, relational level. Jesus explained to
her that there was water he could give her that would ensure
she would never be thirsty again. Of course, she immediately
understood this water to be of great physical and practical help
to her. If she were never thirsty again, she would never have to
suffer the feeling of emptiness and thirst. She would never have
to come to the well to draw water again. No thirst, no fatigue,
no dehydration, no flagging energy as she struggled to lower her

vessel into the well and draw it up again during the hottest part of the day. What Jesus told her, so she thought, was something that could relieve at least some of the inconvenience she now had to experience.

But the point that Jesus was making was not that he had some magic water, as if the woman's greatest need was that she no longer be physically thirsty. Jesus was speaking not about her felt need for water but about the unfelt need that she had for true love and satisfaction. Jesus' point was that this woman had committed her life to water that becomes stale and eventually fails to satisfy. She was drinking the wrong water from the wrong well.

Jeremiah made this point hundreds of years before when he wrote, "For my people have committed two evils: they have forsaken me, the fountain of living waters, and hewed out cisterns for themselves, broken cisterns that can hold no water" (Jer. 2:13). The woman at the well had gone from cistern to cistern, and every one proved to be broken; it could not satisfy. She had determined to meet her felt needs, while ignoring her unfelt need. As is the case in so much of Scripture, Jesus uses physical realities and desires to point to deeper and lasting spiritual realities. Jesus uses the one to point to the other. Her physical thirst pointed to a deeper reality, a deeper need. So it is with us all. Whether we are sixteen or sixty, there is within every one of us this "thirst behind the thirst."

SEE! THE STREAMS OF LIVING WATER

In order for us to understand what Jesus was telling the woman at the well, it may be helpful to see the bigger picture. Jesus tells the woman at the well that he can give her "living water." This "living water" was the Holy Spirit himself. This becomes crystal clear in John 7:

On the last day of the feast, the great day, Jesus stood up and cried out, "If anyone thirsts, let him come to me and drink. Whoever believes in me, as the Scripture has said, 'Out of his heart will flow rivers of living water.'" Now this he said about the Spirit, whom those who believed in him were to receive, for as yet the Spirit had not been given, because Jesus was not yet glorified. (John 7:37–39)

This is a fascinating passage. It requires a little digging for us to get at the root of what John is communicating. There are two central points that John makes here in his inspired commentary on Jesus' words. The first point is obvious, the other, perhaps not so obvious. First, the obvious.

John notes that Jesus' reference to the rivers of living water is a reference to the Holy Spirit. The living waters will flow. That is, they are dynamic, not static. The Holy Spirit is not a *lake* of living water, but a stream or river. The direction of the flow will be from the internal outward. The Spirit will flow *out of* the heart and *into* our daily lives. As Jesus said elsewhere:

The good person out of the good treasure of his heart produces good, and the evil person out of his evil treasure produces evil, for out of the abundance of the heart his mouth speaks. (Luke 6:45)

The "good treasure" of our hearts can only be the Spirit himself, since the heart of man is corrupt apart from the Spirit's regenerating work.

Second, John notes that there is a significant aspect of the Spirit's ministry that can take place only after Jesus is glorified. Those who believed had not yet been given the Spirit, since Jesus had not yet been glorified. To understand what John is telling us, we need to see the point that he makes that is not quite as explicit.

John says, "*for as yet the Spirit had not been given*, because Jesus was not yet glorified" (7:39). This is a helpful translation because it communicates John's intent. But it is not exactly what John says. If this clause were translated literally, it would say, "for the Spirit *was not yet*, because Jesus was not yet glorified." John writes as though the Spirit's very existence was still in the future. It seems as though John wants to say that the Spirit cannot even "be" unless and until Jesus is glorified. Why such a stark statement? Hadn't the Spirit been active throughout history? It may help us to highlight some of the central aspects of the Spirit's work as we find it revealed to us in Holy Scripture.

The Work of the Holy Spirit

In order for us to see why John says the Spirit "was not yet," three related elements of the work of the Holy Spirit need to be emphasized. Fortunately, those elements can all be seen in the first "appearance" of the Holy Spirit in Scripture: Genesis 1:2.

> In the beginning, God created the heavens and the earth. The earth was without form and void, and darkness was over the face of the deep. And the Spirit of God was hovering over the face of the waters. And God said . . . (Gen. 1:1–3)

There is enough packed into this short passage to occupy us for some time. We can highlight only the elements here that immediately concern us. God creates the heavens and the earth, *but he creates them formless and void.* Just exactly why God creates this way is not explained. The fact remains, however, that initially God's creation was confused and empty.

This confusion, or formlessness, and emptiness, or void, should be seen in light of what the rest of this chapter (as well as the rest of Scripture) teaches. God's creation, since it was *God's* creation, could not be completely confused or formless. It was formless in comparison with what it would become. So also, it could not be empty of *everything*, because God himself was there. Rather, it was empty of the light, beauty, and majesty that it would soon have.

What seems clear in this passage, in light of the rest of Scripture, is that in creating the world in this way, God is anticipating the struggle with sin and darkness that would soon ensue because of the fall. In Jeremiah 4, for example, the prophet says:

> How long must I see the standard
> and hear the sound of the trumpet?
>
> "For my people are foolish;
> they know me not;
> they are stupid children;
> they have no understanding.
> They are 'wise'—in doing evil!
> But how to do good they know not."
>
> I looked on the earth, and behold, *it was without form and
> void*;
> and to the heavens, and they had no light. (Jer. 4:21–23)

Jeremiah's reference to Genesis 1:2 has to do with the effects of sin on and in the world (see also Isa. 34:11–15). He illustrates those effects by referring back to the original creation, which was formless and void.

But what happened to this formless and void creation? The

answer to that question will help us see the work of the Spirit in its proper biblical context. The earth, as formless and void, is nevertheless "populated" by the Holy Spirit himself. Genesis tells us that the Holy Spirit is hovering over the face of the waters. From the beginning, therefore, we can trace three central and related aspects of the Spirit's work.

Creator. First, the Spirit himself is active and present in creation as Creator. It is just *because* the Spirit is hovering over the waters that God then speaks his word to *form* what is otherwise formless and *fill* what is otherwise empty: "By the word of the LORD the heavens were made, and by the breath of his mouth all their host" (Ps. 33:6).

The "breath of his mouth" in this case is the Holy Spirit (the Hebrew word translated "breath" here is the same word that translates as "Spirit"). The breath of the Lord's mouth is the Spirit himself (see also Job 26:13). The Holy Spirit, together with the Father and the Son, was active in and for the creation of the world.

Presence. Second, the Spirit of God is active and present *in* creation as Creator. That is, we learn from Genesis 1:2 that the Holy Spirit is the one who is present *with* creation. The picture we have from Genesis 1:2–31 is that as God speaks from above, he speaks his creative word *into* creation, and it is the Spirit himself who is present in creation to apply that word. The Spirit of God, in this case, is the one who comes down to be *in* creation for the purpose of creating. He is the very presence of God in creation.

Echoes of this truth are repeated throughout Scripture. In Genesis 6, for example, as God's patience is wearing thin because of the sinfulness of man, it is the Spirit of God himself who is said to be abiding in man. The Spirit is *in* man because he was the one who gave to man that unique characteristic of being the image of God. It was because God breathed into man the breath of life that he became a living creature (Gen. 2:7). At no other time did God breathe into his creation; only man possesses the breath of God (remember, "breath" and "Spirit" are the same Hebrew word); only man is the image of God.

In Exodus 33:14–17, Moses asks the Lord to be with him. He understands that unless the Lord's presence is with him, there will be no difference between Israel and all the other nations on the face of the earth. This presence of the Lord is the Spirit of the Lord himself.

So also in Psalm 51—that great penitential psalm of David— David prays, "Cast me not away from your presence, and take not your Holy Spirit from me" (Ps. 51:11). David understood that to be cast away from the presence of the Lord is to have the Holy Spirit taken from him. The Spirit *for* the purpose of creation is also the Spirit *in* creation, and in us.

Purifier. Third, Scripture tells us that the Spirit of God was hovering, or brooding, over the face of the waters (Gen. 1:2). The water (sometimes translated "the deep") was that which was in confusion, covering the face of the earth. The deep waters, also referred to in Scripture as the "sea," is that which itself is chaotic, but which also is used for the purpose of cleansing. When the children of Israel were led out of Egypt, it was the (Red) sea that "cleansed" the Lord's people, as it swallowed up the Egyptians (see Ex. 15:8–10). In the book of Revelation, Babylon, that great enemy of the Lord and his people, is cast down into the sea (Rev. 18:21). The sea is the place of chaos and the place that is overcome by God himself in order to set aside, to sanctify and purify, his own people. So chaotic is the sea that the book of Revelation describes that perfect place of purity—the new heavens and the new earth—as a place in which "the sea was no more" (Rev. 21:1).

The Spirit of God is the one who takes the chaos and confusion of "the waters" and tames them, or calms them, for purposes of purification. That which is confused and life-*consuming* becomes cleansing and life-*giving*. One passage that communicates this clearly is Ezekiel 36:25–27:

> I will sprinkle clean water on you, and you shall be clean from all your uncleanesses, and from all your idols I will cleanse you. And I will give you a new heart, and a new spirit I will put within you. And I will remove the heart of stone from your flesh and give you a heart of flesh. And I will put my Spirit within you, and cause you to walk in my statutes and be careful to obey my rules.

From the creation onward, the Spirit is closely linked with aspects of the purifying, life-giving, and cleansing elements of water (Neh. 9:20; Isa. 44:3; Ezek. 36:25).

So, in Genesis 1:2 we begin to see that the Holy Spirit was the *Creator*, applying God's creative word; he was *present in* creation; he was present as the One who *purifies*; he is present for the purpose of *cleansing* and *bringing life* to the chaos and confusion of creation in its initial state.

If this is true, why does the apostle John say in chapter 7 that the Spirit "was not yet"? Surely the Holy Spirit "was" because he had "been" in creation since the beginning. What is John telling us by such stark language? In order to answer that question, we should be aware of just how John interweaves these three notions of the Spirit's *creative* activity, his *presence*, and his *purifying* and *life-giving* power in his gospel.

The Holy Spirit and Jesus' Glorification

In John 2, at a wedding in Cana, Jesus turns water into wine. John tells us that the water was there as preparation for the Jewish rite of purification (John 2:6; see also Lev. 14:51; Num. 8:7; 19:18–22; Ezek. 36:25). The water meant for the Jewish rite of purification was used by Christ for a total *transformation* of this water into something completely different.

This notion of purification is taken up again in the same chapter. Jesus cleanses the temple, making it fit for the *presence* of God. After cleansing the physical temple, Jesus then relates this act to the spiritual temple of his own body (which, in the New Testament, is called the church of Jesus Christ, the temple of God, where the Spirit dwells).

In John 3, the subject of discussion is the new birth. Being born again is a re-*creation* of the Spirit of God. It is a work that the Spirit does *in* us as we become a new creation (see 2 Cor. 5:17). Jesus tells Nicodemus that he must be born "of water and of the Spirit." What could Jesus mean by that?

It seems certain that he was not referring to Christian baptism, since such a thing was not yet instituted. When we keep in mind that he was talking to Nicodemus, a teacher of Israel, there can be little question that what Jesus is referring to is what was embedded in Nicodemus from his childhood. Surely Jesus was referring Nicodemus to the passage above from Ezekiel. This "teacher of Israel" would have immediately called to mind the relationship of water and the Spirit as it is given in that passage. As with the woman at the well, Jesus was using physical realities—birth, water—to point Nicodemus to the more permanent, spiritual realities of a *new* birth and a *true* cleansing.

In John 4, as we saw above, Jesus promises to give "living water" to those who know him (John 4:10). The discussion then turns to the topic of the proper location of the temple (the *presence* of God) and of worship. In chapter 5, Jesus heals the man by the pool of Bethesda; in chapter 6, he walks on water.

Clearly, the apostle John intends to help us see the connection between the creative activity of the Spirit, his presence as he takes up residence in those who belong to Christ, and the spiritual "water" that cleanses and purifies the Christian.

But this still does not answer the question of why John says the Spirit "was not yet." John himself gives us part of the answer. The Spirit "was not yet" because Jesus was not yet glorified. This provides the key to what John means.

If you were asked the question, "What was Jesus' final, redemptive work on earth?" you might be tempted to say, "The resurrection." If we call to mind the words of John the Baptist when he was referring to Christ, we will begin to see the force of the "not yet" of the Spirit's ministry:

> And John bore witness: "I saw the Spirit descend from heaven like a dove, and it remained on him. I myself did not know him, but he who sent me to baptize with water said to me, 'He on whom you see the Spirit descend and remain, this is he who baptizes with the Holy Spirit.' And I have seen and have borne witness that this is the Son of God." (John 1:32–34; see also Matt. 3:11; Mark 1:8; Luke 3:16)

Jesus' final earthly redemptive work, according to John the Baptist, was to send the Holy Spirit at Pentecost and to baptize his people with the Spirit of God. This baptism *by* Jesus *with* the Holy Spirit is a baptism that takes place after Jesus' ascension. In other words, as John tells us in chapter 7, *now that Jesus is glorified*, the Spirit can be given to the church in a way that was not possible until that glorification.

Jesus' victory over death is complete. He has died, has been raised, and is now exalted to the right hand of the Majesty on high (Heb. 1). As Jesus promised, he would not leave us as orphans (John 14:18). He would come to us. He will come to us on that final day. In the meantime, since Jesus has paid the penalty that we deserve and has been glorified by the Father, he comes to us in his Spirit (John 14:23).

In John 7:39, John says the Spirit was not yet given because Pentecost had not yet come. Or, to see how the Spirit's work relates to his activity since creation, just as the Spirit was active as Creator, Presence, and Purifier, so also it is his work, based now on the finished work of Christ, that re-creates us (2 Cor. 5:17; Titus 3:5). Now re-created, we have been indwelt by the Spirit (1 Cor. 6:19) so that we become his temple. As re-created and indwelt Christians, we are holy, purified, and renewed unto knowledge, righteousness, and holiness (1 Cor. 1:30; Col. 3:10; Eph. 4:24). Those who believe in Christ, now that his work on earth is done, receive for eternity the promised Holy Spirit. He purifies us, he makes us his temple, he transforms us, regenerates us, and unites us, eternally, to the Son.

It is the Holy Spirit who saves us from the ebb and flow of uncertainty in this life. It is the Spirit who sets us on the solid ground of certainty. It is the Spirit who gives us "solid joys and lasting treasure." Notice how the apostle Paul reminds us of this:

> In him you also, when you heard the word of truth, the gospel of your salvation, and believed in him, were sealed with the promised Holy Spirit, who is the guarantee of our inheritance until we acquire possession of it, to the praise of his glory. (Eph. 1:13–14)

Most of us may be weary of flimsy promises that never last or guarantees that are never fulfilled. But the guarantee of the

Spirit is different. This guarantee is from God himself. And the presence of the Spirit in us means that our inheritance of eternal life with God is as certain as God himself. What other ground is there that can give us such sure footing? What other promise is so sure? Our future is certain if the Spirit has taken up residence in us. We will live eternally with the Triune God.

This living water, the third person of the Trinity, is the one meant to fill the "God-shaped emptiness" inside us. That *undercurrent* of our unfelt need, which is the knowledge of God that we constantly try to suppress, can become a *spring* of living water only if God the Holy Spirit gives us a new birth. Nothing else can satisfy us; our hearts will remain restless (Augustine), and we will never truly know ourselves (Calvin), unless the undercurrent is transformed into a flowing spring of living water.

Just as the Samaritan woman tried to quench her spiritual thirst (unfelt need) with a series of husbands, people today try a series of popular twenty-first-century thirst-quenchers: power at work, home, church; better houses, cars, or lovers; social acceptance by wealth, appearance, or connections. The gospel reminds us that true satisfaction will not be found by fulfilling our true desires by means of "finding ourselves" and then meeting our needs by our own efforts. Like the woman of Samaria, we come to recognize the real need for living water only when Jesus brings it to our attention.

We should be careful to note here the stark contrast between the way that we typically try to meet our needs and the way that Christ does. Our solutions are always only temporary. Like the woman at the well we move from one commitment to the next, hoping all the while that we will finally be satisfied.

But the point that Jesus is making is that our true need is not physical water, or husbands, or pleasure, or . . . Our true need is for a permanent solution, one that does not ebb and flow with the times, one not subject to the whims and wishes of our fickle hearts. We need living water; we need permanent change; we need the Holy Spirit to unite us to Christ. In him we have the true Bread (John 6:32) and living water, so that we will never be *truly* hungry or thirsty again. All of our needs are met in him, because, in the end, our only real need is to be united to Christ, by the Spirit.

WATER WELLING UP

It should not escape our notice that when Jesus discusses the living water in chapters 4 and 7 of John's gospel, he uses very active verbs. In John 4:14, he speaks of this living water as "welling up to eternal life." In John 7:38, the water "flows" out of us. In other words, the work of the Spirit *in* us is meant to express itself *out of* us; it is meant to "well up" so that, like a spring, it moves from the inside out.

In chapter 1 we looked briefly at the opening verses in the book of Hebrews. The book itself, as we might expect, is written to Christians. Even so, it is full of serious warnings to those who claim to have experienced the living water of Christ, but who show no signs of life. In that sense, Hebrews is a book that highlights the point that living water is meant to *flow*, it is intended to *well up* to eternal life. Hebrews reminds us that holiness is not an option for a Christian; it is an essential element of our transformation. Without holiness, no one will see the Lord (Heb. 12:14).

The author to the Hebrews highlights the same themes that we have been discussing. Speaking of the house of God, he says,

> Let us draw near with a true heart in full assurance of faith, with our hearts sprinkled clean from an evil conscience and our

bodies washed with pure water. Let us hold fast the confession of our hope without wavering, for he who promised is faithful. And let us consider how to stir up one another to love and good works. (Heb. 10:22–24)

Notice that the reality of our hearts being cleansed moves the author almost immediately to an exhortation of service to others. To put it in more common vernacular, the author is saying that since our needs have all been met, we should turn our consideration to others. Here the author is thinking about others within the household of faith. But Jesus reminds us that our responsibilities reach further than that.

Jesus uses a story about another Samaritan to illustrate the proper reaction of those whose needs have been met in him, those who have been washed with living water (Luke 10:25–37). A lawyer, most likely an authority in God's law, asked Jesus how a man could inherit eternal life. Jesus said, "You shall love the Lord your God with all your heart and with all your soul and with all your strength and with all your mind, and your neighbor as yourself." The lawyer asked, "And who is my neighbor?"

Instead of replying directly, Jesus told the story that has come to be known as "The Good Samaritan." The Samaritan man—again, one who was hated by the Jewish community—was a man who exhibited great self-denial in interrupting his own journey in order to help a man who had been beaten, robbed, and most likely left for dead. The Samaritan was not the first person to come upon the victim. Jesus relates that both a priest and a Levite passed the wounded traveler and moved to the other side of the road without offering any assistance. The Samaritan not only stopped and treated the injured man's wounds, but he also put the man on his own donkey, took him to an inn, and left money for the man's care until he recovered. The Samaritan even promised to pay more money to the innkeeper, should it be needed, upon his return trip.

Jesus then asked the expert in the law, "Which of these three, do you think, proved to be a neighbor to the man who fell among the robbers?" The answer: "The one who showed him mercy." In telling this parable, Jesus shows the lawyer that his question was misplaced. The question is not, who is my neighbor? The question is, am I a neighbor to those who cross my path? The living water that is ours in Christ is meant to well up to those around me. Because of this eternal, living water, *I* am a neighbor, and that means that any who come into contact with me are meant to have their own thirst quenched by that water. In meeting our most basic need, the Lord calls us to tend to the needs of others. Am I willing to be a neighbor, to be the one who shows mercy to others?

Where do we place ourselves in the parable of the good Samaritan? Most likely, we do not want to see ourselves as the victim of robbers, helpless, left to die. Part of Jesus' point was that often religious people are like the priest and the Levite who passed by on the other side of the road in order to avoid becoming unclean or inconvenienced. The fact is, we are meant to relate to two key players in the parable. If we have come to Christ, we know that we were like the wounded man. We were helpless and dying, until Jesus showed mercy. Jesus saw the need and fulfilled it.

But now that Jesus has met our most basic need, we are to be like the good Samaritan. We are to be those who, because God has loved us (and, therefore, we love him), show that love to those who themselves need Christ—those who are wounded and broken, and who cannot help themselves.

Suppose a young Christian woman is struggling with unmet needs for love and acceptance. Perhaps she is at a large university and is having difficulty finding friends and establishing meaningful relationships, even within the Christian groups she seeks out. She has not been invited to pledge a sorority and is convinced it is because she doesn't drive a nice enough car or wear designer clothes.

Perhaps there is a personality problem. She is such an introvert that it is painful to initiate conversations with others. In all these areas, she feels shortchanged. She may even feel resentful or angry with God and then angry with other Christians who seem to be more blessed than she. She waits for God to do something, to send friends and relationships her way, to give her a financial break, to change her personality to one that will attract others.

How does the gospel apply to her life? Why is the living water not satisfying her thirst? How does this affect the young college student? Does she see herself as one who needed God's mercy and the work of Jesus or as a good person who deserves the attention and love of God and others? Understanding our own need of living water and how Jesus has fulfilled that need will bring forth a rush of compassion and mercy for others (John 7:38). Why are we not compassionate? What will change us? Is it not the living water that springs up in us?

The gospel impacts our relationships. As we grow in grace, selfishness gives way to self-denial. Why? Because the Good Samaritan (Jesus) has shown compassion to us; he has healed our wounds as he was "wounded for our transgressions." He has paid (by his own blood) for our restoration. The living water enables us to love, to consider the interests of others greater than our own, to forgive, and to take the initiative in reconciliation.

WHO CAN FAINT?

In the midst of the affirmation of the springs of living water, Newton asks the question, "Who can faint while such a river ever flows their thirst t'assuage?" If, indeed, we have been given "streams of living water," then we have the Holy Spirit. If we have the Holy Spirit, then, as Newton reminds us, all fear of want is removed.

Who, then, *can* faint? If the living river of the Holy Spirit ever flows in us, then our thirst is, from that time forward and into eternity, assuaged. All the felt needs that we have, Christ has promised to meet, in his own time and his own way. That is the case because our only unfelt need, our need for fellowship with the living God, has been met in him.

This is the gospel of God's saving grace. It re-creates us, it blesses us with his holy presence within us, and it cleanses and purifies us so that, in Christ, we are acceptable in his sight. This grace will never fail, because the God of grace will never fail. All our needs are eternally supplied in the certainty of his loving grace.

Grace, which, like the Lord, the giver,
Never fails from age to age.

DISCUSSION QUESTIONS

1. Describe a time in your life when you were actively trying to discover who you are/were.
2. Read Genesis 3:1–11. In the garden of Eden, God asked Adam and Eve, "Where are you?" God was questioning not their physical location but the location of the desires of their hearts. How do you view your vertical relationship with God? Where is your heart right now? How do you try to hide from God?
3. What are the ramifications of being made in the image of God, but without Christ, still in our sin? Is this an excuse for immoral behavior?

4. When Jesus spoke to the woman at the well, he was speaking "not about her felt need for water, but about the unfelt need that she had for true love and satisfaction." What is the water we use to quench our thirst daily?

5. How have you exchanged the truth you know to be true of Christ for images of created things?

6. What is the "good treasure" of our hearts, as mentioned in Luke 6:45?

7. What are the three related elements of the work of the Holy Spirit?

8. Read Luke 10:25–37. Where do you see yourself in the parable of the good Samaritan? How are you a neighbor to those who cross your path?

3: WE ARE NOT ALONE

ROUND EACH HABITATION HOVERING

Round each habitation hovering,
See the cloud and fire appear!
For a glory and a covering,
Showing that the Lord is near:
Thus deriving from their banner
Light by night, and shade by day;
Safe they feed upon the manna
Which he gives them when they pray.

This great stanza of this magnificent hymn urges a number of crucial truths upon us. It points us to our Lord's faithfulness, to his loving guidance of his people throughout history, and to his abundant provision. There is one particular truth, however, that underlies all the rest. It is a truth that may be obvious to us, but can be difficult to grasp fully. It is the glorious truth of God's holy presence with his people. We hinted at this in our last chapter; we need to think a bit more about it here.

At the end of Shakespeare's final play, *The Tempest*, Prospero comes to grips with the fact that his twisted and conflicted servant, Caliban, is someone whom he finally must reckon with. Prospero recognizes that Caliban is his responsibility. "This thing of darkness," he says, "I acknowledge mine."[1] And while Prospero is referring directly to Caliban, scholars of Shakespeare have little doubt that the lesson here is that "this thing of darkness" is the tempest that rages in the heart of man. "This thing of darkness" is something that belongs to every one of us who is born in Adam.

If we know anything of Scripture, we know that the heart of man is in many ways a thing of mystery, of darkness. But we also know that since Adam and Eve fell in the garden, "this thing of darkness" is almost unbounded in its capacity for evil. The first mention of the heart in Scripture is Genesis 6:5: "The LORD saw that the wickedness of man was great in the earth, and that every intention of the thoughts of his heart was only evil continually." The reason for this wickedness, at least in part, is that our hearts convince us that we can get along well without God, that we know how to run our own lives by ourselves. In Adam, we profess ourselves to be wise, though Scripture assures us that our foolish hearts are darkened (Rom. 1:21).

But what does this darkness look like? Generally speaking, of course, it looks like sin. But one of the reasons that Scripture speaks of sin as darkness is that it is, in all of its forms, an attempt to move away from the true light of God's holy presence. In other words, sin is an attempt (though futile) to hide from the God who is ever-present. We have already noticed the response of our first parents after they had sinned and realized that God was in the garden. What did they do?

And they heard the sound of the LORD God walking in the garden in the cool of the day, and the man and his wife hid

1. Shakespeare, *The Tempest*, 5.1.

themselves from the presence of the LORD God among the trees of the garden. (Gen. 3:8)

It would be fortunate for us, as Christians, if this kind of foolishness were reserved for those who are outside the church, those who have no knowledge of the gospel and of its benefits. But Scripture indicates that such is not the case:

"Woe to the shepherds who destroy and scatter the sheep of my pasture!" declares the LORD. Therefore thus says the LORD, the God of Israel, concerning the shepherds who care for my people: "You have scattered my flock and have driven them away, and you have not attended to them. Behold, I will attend to you for your evil deeds, declares the LORD." . . .

Thus says the LORD of hosts: "Do not listen to the words of the prophets who prophesy to you, filling you with vain hopes. They speak visions of their own minds, not from the mouth of the LORD. They say continually to those who despise the word of the LORD, 'It shall be well with you'; and to everyone who stubbornly follows his own heart, they say, 'No disaster shall come upon you.'"

For who among them has stood in the council of the LORD
    to see and to hear his word,
    or who has paid attention to his word and listened? . . .

I did not send the prophets,
    yet they ran;
I did not speak to them,
    yet they prophesied.
But if they had stood in my council,
    then they would have proclaimed my words to my people,

and they would have turned them from their evil way,
　　and from the evil of their deeds.

Am I a God at hand, declares the LORD, and not a God far
away? *Can a man hide himself in secret places so that I cannot see
him? declares the LORD.* Do I not fill heaven and earth? declares
the LORD. (Jer. 23:1–2, 16–18, 21–24)

The leaders of Israel in Jeremiah's day had apparently convinced themselves that they could hide themselves from God,
that the sins they were bent on committing, since they were
done in "secret," were hidden from all, even from God. They
had convinced themselves that they had found places to which
even God could not go.

HOME ALONE?

There are cultural conditions that arise in history that seem
to provide a more comfortable context for certain kinds of sins.
For example, one of the things that the Enlightenment was able
to do was to provide a context in which men and women could
become overly optimistic about their own abilities to reason
rightly and to handle their own problems. In various ways and
degrees, the church fell prey to that way of thinking as well. For
example, arguments for the fallibility of Scripture began to fall
on more fertile soil. Such arguments (in spite of postmodernism's
attempts to refute the Enlightenment) have only gained support.

In the same way, it appears that the cultural climate today,
especially (in some ways) in the West, has given rise to forms
of darkness that were in other times more difficult to create.
How did we get here? What particular forms of darkness present
themselves today? To the first question first.

There are some historical and cultural "signals" that might help us see our current situation in its proper context. In the world of philosophy, some of the unique problems we face today reached their pinnacle in the thinking of Immanuel Kant (1724–1804). Kant argued that the world we live in is a world of our own making, that we are each responsible for our own worlds. Though his ideas were concocted in the ivory tower, they began to grow legs and walk the streets. So influential were Kant's ideas that Alan Bloom could say, in *The Closing of the American Mind*, that every entering college student came to college with one bedrock assumption. That assumption is that "truth is relative." This is Kant's legacy to us. Since the world I live in is the world I create, truth can only be my truth—it can only be "true for me."[2]

But Kant's legacy has taken on new forms that have been fed by new opportunities for sin, opportunities that were not as extensive and as available in days gone by. Some of Kant's most dangerous ideas have found a resting place in some of our latest and greatest conveniences. Perhaps we can illustrate this by way of another philosopher, Jean Paul Sartre (1905–1980).

Sartre was an atheist who committed himself to a search for the meaning of existence (not a promising task for an atheist to undertake). In his search for individual meaning, Sartre was convinced that one of the main threats to such meaning was the existence of other people.

To illustrate this, Sartre used the example of a man staring through the keyhole of a door. For Sartre, no matter what one saw through that keyhole, or why one was looking, the simple, individual act of one looking through a keyhole was "judgment-free." No one was there, so there was no accountability.

---

2. Alan Bloom, *The Closing of the American Mind* (New York: Simon & Schuster, 1987), 25.

The act itself was neither good nor evil. How could it be, since it was carried out by an individual? Surely, no one was hurt and there were no victims.

But then, says Sartre, the man looking through the keyhole hears footsteps in the hall. Suddenly, he becomes embarrassed. He is conscious of his act and begins to evaluate it according to what "the Other" might think of it and of him.

Sartre detests the presence of "the Other." Other people always impose on us constraints that would not be there if they weren't there. Apart from their presence, there is no right or wrong behavior. In Sartre's own infamous words—"No one can be vulgar all alone."[3]

Sartre expanded on this idea. In his play, *No Exit*, he concludes, "Hell is other people."[4] In his novel, *Nausea*, Sartre's "hero," Roquentin, says, "I live alone, entirely alone. I never speak to anyone, never; I receive nothing, I give nothing."[5]

Kant's "Individual," who creates his own world, has become Sartre's "I," whose individual actions are without concern or consequence, as long as one can ensure that whatever is done, is done alone, as an individual.

These ideas of individualism have been supported in other ways as well. Think of the "Heisenberg principle" of quantum physics. According to Niels Bohr, quantum reality is in part an observer-created reality. One physicist, John A. Wheeler, said, "No elementary phenomenon is a phenomenon until it is an observed phenomenon." This is Kant and Sartre applied to science. Now

3. Jean-Paul Sartre, *Being and Nothingness*, trans. Hazel Barnes (n.p.: Citadel Press, 2001), 198.

4. Jean-Paul Sartre, *No Exit* in *Four Contemporary French Plays*, trans. Stuart Gilbert (New York: Random House, 1967), 111.

5. Jean-Paul Sartre, *Nausea*, trans. Lloyd Alexander (New York: New Directions, 1964), 14.

it seems human observations "influence" the structure of the physical world.

Or, think of the movie by the Coen brothers entitled, *The Man Who Wasn't There*. Ed, the barber, is the man who wasn't there. Ed is accused of murder. His lawyer, in the end, wants to argue that the jury should take a hard look at the meaning of the facts. He is convinced they will realize that the facts have no meaning. This is the movie version of the Heisenberg principle.

The cultural critic, Robert Bellah, has argued in his book, *Habits of the Heart*, that the quintessential habits of American hearts relate directly to our individualism. One example he gives that perhaps we don't normally see is automobiles.[6]

Why is it that we can so easily become perturbed or angry when we are driving? One reason must be that we consider ourselves to be "king of the road" when we drive. We assume that the road is ours for the taking, and woe be to anyone who causes us to in any way modify our behavior. This is a good illustration of individualism run amok in our culture.

From philosophy to movies to cars, the clear message that is presented to us is that we make our own rules, determine our own behavior, and are ruled by no one but ourselves in the process.

Think of these influences, now, in the context of inventions more recent, and potentially more insidious, than the automobile: the television and the computer. Neither of these things is bad in itself. If we are not careful to recognize their dangers, however, they can be devastating to the pursuit of holiness. If we don't keep a critical eye on them, these objects can combine to form the "perfect storm" of presumed individualism

6. Robert N. Bellah, Richard Madsen, William M. Sullivan, Ann Swidler, and Steven M. Tipton, *Habits of the Heart: Individualism and Commitment in American Life* (Berkeley, CA: University of California Press, 1985).

and isolation, a storm that can wreak havoc when not properly checked with a biblical mindset that is intent on holiness and on pleasing God. Given these disparate influences, we have a ready-made context—one that is so much a part of our daily lives that we may hardly even think about it—for the propagation and instigation of all kinds of dark and private sins.

Perhaps it is time to ask ourselves if we have agreed, at least in practice, with Sartre's statement. Have we convinced ourselves that, with regard to what we watch on television and what we access on our computers, "no one can be vulgar all alone"? With the scandals in the church related to sexual sin and pornography, surely some have deceived themselves into thinking (like Adam and Jonah) that they can hide from God. Our dark hearts can dupe us into thinking that we really can isolate and insulate ourselves from God's presence, that we can put ourselves into situations where we are in isolation and darkness and where no "light," especially no light of God, can be found.

How can it happen, for example, that a Christian can live like a Christian in public, perhaps preach in a pulpit, but in private fall prey to all kinds of sin and perversion? Part of the answer must be that we can convince ourselves that when we are alone, we are really alone. Like Sartre, the atheist, we can convince ourselves that there is no God, at least not when we are alone.

But we are never "home alone." There is never a time for any of us, and certainly not for Christians, when the eyes of a holy God are closed to our activities and our thoughts. "And no creature is hidden from his sight, but all are naked and exposed to the eyes of him to whom we must give account" (Heb. 4:13). The Lord is always and everywhere present with and for his people. Not only is the Lord present with his people, but he is present in his people, too.

This internal presence of the Lord is something we might be tempted to forget or suppress. The near omnipresence of the cultural influences mentioned above might overrule what we know biblically to be true. But we should remind ourselves of Scripture's clear teaching on this:

> For you, you only, know the hearts of the children of mankind. (2 Chron. 6:30)

> He who teaches man knowledge—the LORD—knows the thoughts of man. (Ps. 94:10–11)

> Every way of a man is right in his own eyes, but the LORD weighs the heart. (Prov. 21:2)

> But Jesus on his part did not entrust himself to them, because he knew all people and needed no one to bear witness about man, for he himself knew what was in man. (John 2:24–25)

> For who knows a person's thoughts except the spirit of that person, which is in him? So also no one comprehends the thoughts of God except the Spirit of God. (1 Cor. 2:11)

> For the word of God is living and active, sharper than any two-edged sword, piercing to the division of soul and of spirit, of joints and of marrow, and discerning the thoughts and intentions of the heart. (Heb. 4:12)

Clearly, the Lord is privy to all of our private thoughts, intentions, and conversations. As Psalm 139 reminds us, this exhaustive knowledge that the Lord has of us is meant to be an occasion for praise. It is a part of his incomprehensible majesty.

Even before a word is on my tongue,
    behold, O Lord, you know it altogether.
You hem me in, behind and before,
    and lay your hand upon me.
Such knowledge is too wonderful for me;
    it is high; I cannot attain it. (Ps. 139:4–6)

But if there are areas of our hearts that remain dark toward God, if we attempt to run from his light in our inmost being, and if we fool ourselves into thinking that we really can be alone, then the knowledge that God has of our hearts is a threat to us, it challenges our pretended autonomy, and it imposes itself on our pretense.

The intimate and exhaustive presence of the Lord is meant to be our greatest blessing. It is our guarantee against loneliness; it fulfills our longing to be accepted and loved. To think biblically about the Lord's presence is to put to death those dark and hidden places of our hearts in order that the light of the gospel might overpower us. It is, in effect, to surrender ourselves wholly—both externally and internally—to God.

What exactly does this exhaustive presence of the Lord mean for those of us who are his people? We catch a sense of what it means in Exodus 33. Just after Israel had disobeyed the Lord by making and worshiping the golden calf, the Lord tells Moses that he must remove his presence from them lest he consume them on the way. In other words, the wrath of the Lord burns against Israel to the extent that the Lord's own presence has turned from a blessing to a curse.

But Moses pleads with the Lord, and the Lord relents:

Moses said to the Lord, "See, you say to me, 'Bring up this people,' but you have not let me know whom you will send with me. Yet you have said, 'I know you by name, and you have also found favor in my sight.' Now therefore, if I have found favor in your sight, please show me now your ways, that I may know you in order to find favor in your sight. Consider too that this nation is your people." And he said, "My presence will go with you, and I will give you rest." And he said to him, "If your presence will not go with me, do not bring us up from here. For how shall it be known that I have found favor in your sight, I and your people? Is it not in your going with us, so that we are distinct, I and your people, from every other people on the face of the earth?" (Ex. 33:12–16)

Notice in this interchange that there is a connection between the intimacy of Moses' relationship to the Lord and the Lord's recommitment to be present with him. It is because the Lord knows Moses intimately ("I know you by name") and because Moses has been given the grace of God in salvation ("you have also found favor in my sight") that the Lord promises to be with Moses as he leads his people to the Promised Land. The presence of the Lord with his people is a sign of his forgiveness and his intimate love; it is a presence based on his gracious love. It is a family presence.

Note also, however, just what the presence of the Lord means, according to Moses:

For how shall it be known that I have found favor in your sight, I and your people? Is it not in your going with us, so that we are distinct, I and your people, from every other people on the face of the earth? (v. 16)

It is the presence of God that makes the people of God distinct from all the other people on the face of the earth. This is a glorious truth, and we will look below at some ways the Lord's presence distinguishes the Lord's people. This "distinctness" that is a defining characteristic of the Lord's people is not simply something external, as if all that God's presence does is change us outwardly. It is an inward distinctness flowing from an internal change, a change of heart. As a matter of fact, it is just the internal, inward activity that gives evidence of who we really are. "As in water face reflects face, so the heart of man reflects the man" (Prov. 27:19; cf. Matt. 15:19; Mark 7:21).

We should not miss the central and radical truth that is expressed in this distinct presence of God, especially as that truth reaches its marvelous fulfillment in the New Testament. As we saw in chapter 2, because of Christ's finished work, the Holy Spirit, as our "streams of living water," lives within those who are, by faith, in Christ. So central is that truth that the apostle Paul refers to Christians as "a temple of the Holy Spirit" (1 Cor. 6:19). The presence of the Lord—that presence that defined the character of the Lord's people in the Old Testament—is now complete in us, because the work of Christ for our redemption is complete. If the saints of the Old Testament were distinct because of God's holy presence with them, how much more are we, the temple of the Holy Spirit, meant to be distinct from those in whom the Spirit of holiness has now taken up eternal residence?

To understand the intensity of God's holy presence with us is to move a long way toward subduing "this thing of darkness" that remains in us (see Rom. 7:14–25). It is to keep in the forefront of our minds that, wherever we are and whatever we do, God himself is with and in us. So intimate is this presence of God that Paul can argue that we bring Christ himself into our sins when we choose to disobey him (1 Cor. 6:15–20).

We stand, always and everywhere, in the presence of God. And the good news of the gospel is that "this thing of darkness" has been supernaturally and radically transformed in Christ, so that we never need live in darkness again. "For God, who said, 'Let light shine out of darkness,' has shone in our hearts to give the light of the knowledge of the glory of God in the face of Jesus Christ" (2 Cor. 4:6). The same God who took the dark, formless, empty stuff of creation and said, "Let there be light," is the one who has now shone in "this thing of darkness" to give us the light of the knowledge of the glory of God in the face of Jesus Christ.

So, says Paul, while we must not delude ourselves into thinking that we can hide from God, we must just as energetically understand that the only hiding that Christians now pursue is a hiding under the shadow of God's wings (Pss. 36:7; 57:1). In other words, we do not attempt to hide from the presence of God because of our sin, but we revel in his presence because of what Christ has done.

To put this in the context of our discussion, the glorious truth of the gospel is this: The Lord Jesus himself, not with respect to his heart, but with respect to ours, has said, "This thing of darkness I acknowledge mine." He took the sinfulness of our hearts to himself on the cross, so that we would not have to bear the consequences that such sinfulness would otherwise inevitably bring us (more on that in the next chapter). Because he did that great work, because redemption is accomplished by him, his Holy Spirit now applies that redemption to his people and is now with and in them as he creates in them new and holy hearts. As we will see (and as Newton reminds us), he is in us both to guide and to provide.

A MOST SPECIAL MANNER

The providence of God, according to the Westminster Confession of Faith, is that activity whereby he "does uphold, direct, dispose, and govern all creatures, actions, and things, from the greatest even to the least" (WCF 5.1). The apostle Paul refers to this general providence as a testimony of God's goodness to all people and even as a reason why all men should repent before him (see Acts 14:15–17). As important as it is for us to understand this general providence of God, it is equally important to understand God's *special* providence:

> As the providence of God does, in general, reach to all creatures; so, after a most special manner, it takes care of his church, and disposes all things to the good thereof. (WCF 5.7)

The "most special manner" of God's providence for his church includes the remarkable way in which God has determined to bring us closer to himself.

One of the most obvious illustrations of the special *presence* of God with his people and of his special providence is seen both in the guidance and in the provision of food that God made for Israel as they meandered their way through the wilderness:

> And the LORD went before them by day in a pillar of cloud to lead them along the way, and by night in a pillar of fire to give them light, that they might travel by day and by night. The pillar of cloud by day and the pillar of fire by night did not depart from before the people. (Ex. 13:21–22)

The Lord's presence was obvious in the clear guidance that he gave to his people as they left the bondage of Egypt and made their way to the Promised Land. The Lord was with them, and his presence guided them in the way that they should go.

But the Lord's presence also meant that they would receive

not simply a general provision of food, but a provision of food by way of God's special providence to them:

> Then the LORD said to Moses, "Behold, I am about to rain bread from heaven for you, and the people shall go out and gather a day's portion every day, that I may test them, whether they will walk in my law or not. On the sixth day, when they prepare what they bring in, it will be twice as much as they gather daily." So Moses and Aaron said to all the people of Israel, "At evening you shall know that it was the LORD who brought you out of the land of Egypt, and in the morning you shall see the glory of the LORD, because he has heard your grumbling against the LORD. For what are we, that you grumble against us?" And Moses said, "When the LORD gives you in the evening meat to eat and in the morning bread to the full, because the LORD has heard your grumbling that you grumble against him—what are we? Your grumbling is not against us but against the LORD." (Ex. 16:4–8)

This is an extraordinary special providence, especially given the sinful complaints of Israel:

> And the whole congregation of the people of Israel grumbled against Moses and Aaron in the wilderness, and the people of Israel said to them, "Would that we had died by the hand of the LORD in the land of Egypt, when we sat by the meat pots and ate bread to the full, for you have brought us out into this wilderness to kill this whole assembly with hunger." (Ex. 16:2–3)

The Lord determined to provide for Israel in spite of their complaints against him. It could even be said that the Lord determined to provide for Israel so that their complaining and grumbling could be seen for what it is, that is, sin in the presence of God.

There are deep and abiding spiritual truths embedded in this account of God's remarkable guidance and providence. Unless we understand those truths, and they abide in us, however, we will rob ourselves of the blessedness that should be a natural part of living in the presence of God.

What is it that God was doing in guiding Israel and in providing bread for his people in the wilderness? To think that God was concerned only about Israel's location and physical needs is to miss the purpose of his gracious providence toward them. The purpose of God's special providence to Israel in this case was to test his people (Ex. 16:4). The Lord was interested not simply in directing and feeding his people (though he was certainly interested in that), but in the responses that they would give to him as he provided for their physical needs.

THIS IS A TEST

And you shall remember the whole way that the LORD your God has led you these forty years in the wilderness, that he might humble you, testing you to know what was in your heart, whether you would keep his commandments or not. (Deut. 8:2)

The leading and guiding, the feeding and providing of the Lord in "a most special manner" in the wilderness was meant to be a test. It was meant to show whether or not Israel was wholeheartedly committed to the Lord who delivered her. It was meant to demonstrate the true state of Israel's heart. It was a special providence designed to show if there was, indeed, a relationship of heartfelt obedience present between the Lord and his people, or if their relationship to him was only skin-deep.

WE ARE NOT ALONE

It may strike us as strange, at least initially, that the above passage indicates that the Lord tests us so that he might know what is in our hearts. This truth is expressed elsewhere in Scripture, perhaps most strikingly in the Lord's testing of Abraham in Genesis 22. Abraham is commanded to sacrifice his only son. He is fully prepared to obey that command, trusting the Lord's faithfulness in the midst of his trial (Heb. 11:17–18). But the Lord intervenes; he does not allow Abraham to finish the task. And the reason given?

> Do not lay your hand on the boy or do anything to him, *for now I know that you fear God*, seeing you have not withheld your son, your only son, from me. (Gen. 22:12)

The reason for Abraham's test was so that the Lord would know that Abraham feared God. How could this be? Isn't the Lord himself omniscient, knowing all things completely and from eternity?

We miss the point of this passage, and others like it, if we think that what the Lord is after here is bare knowledge. We dare not think the Lord acts in history in order to be apprised of facts that are otherwise hidden from him. The Lord is never in need of an education. As we have already seen, the Lord knows the heart of man; he knows our going out and our coming in. He knows us intimately, even from the time of our conception. He knew us, in eternity, before we, or anything else in creation, existed. What, then, do these passages mean that tell us that the testings we endure are given to us so the Lord may know how we might react to them?

It may help us to remember that oftentimes when Scripture speaks of "knowledge" or "to know," it speaks not of new information being imparted to the brain, but rather of a new or closer intimacy in a relationship. Note, for example, "Now Adam knew Eve his wife, and she conceived" (Gen. 4:1). Obviously, Scripture is not telling us here that Eve conceived by virtue of Adam's gaining new information about her. The "knowing" of Adam toward Eve was an intimate, relational knowing.

So it is with the Lord in his covenant relationship to his people. The "knowledge" that the Lord gains through the testing of Abraham, of Israel, and of us is the intimate knowledge that just is our relationship to him. When the Lord says, as a result of testing, "Now I know . . . ," he is not saying that new information has been given to him that otherwise would have been hidden from his sight. Rather, he is saying in effect, "Now the depth of your heart commitment to me has been revealed in your actions."

In other words, the testing of the Lord is designed to strip away all superficiality and to get to the root of our commitment to him. It is meant to show just what the relationship that he has sovereignly established with us will look like.

Of course, Israel did not pass the test. In the midst of the Lord's special providence to guide and to provide, Israel grumbled and complained; the people longed to go back to their condition of slavery (see Num. 11). Though they might have acknowledged God outwardly, they would not respond in faith and obedience to his gracious presence.

The book of Hebrews summarizes the disobedience of Israel's wilderness wandering in stark terms:

Therefore, as the Holy Spirit says,

"Today, if you hear his voice,
do not harden your hearts as in the rebellion,
    on the day of testing in the wilderness,
where your fathers put me to the test
    and saw my works for forty years.

Therefore I was provoked with that generation,
and said, 'They always go astray in their heart;
   they have not known my ways.'
As I swore in my wrath,
   'They shall not enter my rest.'" (Heb. 3:7–11)

The first generation of those who were brought out of their slavery in Egypt did not enter the Promised Land. That in itself was tragic. But the deeper tragedy goes beyond the physical land. The deeper tragedy is displayed in that in God's testing of Israel, no faith or obedience was found: "And to whom did he swear that they would not enter his rest, but to those who were disobedient? So we see that they were unable to enter because of unbelief" (Heb. 3:18–19).

Israel's wandering in the wilderness was to test their own hearts. It was the context that the Lord designed to illustrate not what Israel said about their relationship to the Lord, but what Israel did in response to the relationship that the Lord had established.

But the crucial lesson for us is that Israel's test took place not in the depths of their slavery in Egypt. They were not tested and tried by the Lord when in their misery. Rather, the Lord had delivered them, guided them by fire and a cloud, and provided for them with daily manna. It was in the context of this special providence and guidance that the testing of the Lord's people took place.

In other words, the testing of the Lord happens to those who have been given the blessings of a covenant relationship to him. The Lord tests those who claim to be his, and he tests them to see if those claims prove to be true. Testing takes place in a context of God's special care of us. As Newton put it, safe they feed upon the manna. And though they were safe from the shackles of Egypt and given daily food from the Lord himself, they perished because of unbelief.

BREAD OF HEAVEN

It may be tempting for us to blame Israel for such blatant ingratitude. When we see how clearly the Lord guided and directed them and how miraculously he rescued and fed them, we might think that their unbelief and disobedience is well-nigh incomprehensible. How could a people, so abundantly and graciously guided and provided for, rebel against the One whose presence was so obvious to them? How could they forget his mercies to them? How could they long for the chains of Egypt as they ate of the bounty of heaven each day?

We might also be tempted to think that if we had the benefit of the fire and cloud to guide us and of the manna from heaven to feed us, then our Christian lives would be filled with nothing but gratitude and mercy because of the obvious presence of the Lord with us each day. If only the Lord would guide and provide for us in the same way that he did for Israel.

But to think in this way is to think as those who misunderstand the reality of redemption in Christ. In his marvelous book, *Called to the Ministry*, Edmund Clowney reminds us of the Lord's new covenant mode of guidance and provision:

> There are times when we may wish that one of the old "divers manners" of revelation was still in effect. The Urim and Thummim, for example, were consulted by the priest to secure "yes" or "no" answers from God (Ex. 28:30; I Sam. 28:6). Would you be tempted to trade in the New Testament for the priests' ephod and to find your "yes" and "no" in miraculous stones rather than in Christ? . . .

Knowing the will of the Lord in the fellowship of Jesus Christ is not a technique to provide a substitute for the Urim-Thummim in securing infallible on-the-spot decisions from God. The Lord has not promised to give this, and what he does give you is far better. In his Word, he reveals the principles of his will—indeed, he reveals himself. Through his Spirit he quickens your understanding of his will and your living fellowship with himself.[1]

The point is that because Christ has come, has finished his work, and has sent his Holy Spirit to indwell us, we have the kind of guidance and provision that the Old Testament saints could only dream about. The fire and the cloud, the Urim and Thummim, the manna from heaven—these things were only signs of what was to come. And, from the perspective of God's redemption of his people in history, the best was yet to come. And the best has come: it has come in Christ.

We saw this more clearly when we looked (in chapter 1) at that other testing that took place in the wilderness. Just as soon as Jesus was set apart for his redemptive task, he was immediately led by the Spirit into the wilderness to be tempted (see Matt. 4:1–11; Luke 4:1–13, Mark 1:12–13). Unlike Israel, Jesus had no food from heaven. For forty days and forty nights he was without basic physical necessities.

When the Devil came to tempt Jesus, he foolishly thought that Jesus' greatest need would be for food. If he could only get Jesus to agree with him, then the need for spiritual food would take a backseat to his physical needs, and the Devil would have his victory.

But, unlike Israel, Jesus did not fail the test. Though hungry, he understood that it is the Word of God, the True Manna from

1. Edmund Clowney, *Called to the Ministry* (Phillipsburg, NJ: P&R, 1976), 70–71.

WE ARE NOT ALONE

heaven, that is the need of the hour. Jesus understood that it was not the manna given to Israel that gave them life. True life was found only in the Word of God. True life for us is only found in Christ himself, the true bread from heaven:

> Jesus then said to them, "Truly, truly, I say to you, it was not Moses who gave you the bread from heaven, but my Father gives you the true bread from heaven. For the bread of God is he who comes down from heaven and gives life to the world." (John 6:32–33)

The reality for those who are in Christ, who profess his name, and who are committed to growth in grace is that we have more guidance and more provision for our spiritual journey in the wilderness toward the Promised Land than any of the Lord's people had in the Old Testament. The question for us, in our pursuit of holiness, is this: do we safely feed upon the manna? Have we made "every word that proceeds from the mouth of God" our daily diet? Does the guidance and special providence of God's Word to his church, together with his presence in us, define our very lives?

GOT MILK?

One of the more confusing predicaments in the western church is the disparity between a rise in evangelical faith and the continued moral downturn in western society as a whole. Many are now saying that when it comes to sexual sins and the breakup of families, the percentages in the evangelical church are on a par with those in society at large. What could be the cause of this disparity?

In his first epistle to a group of dislocated Christians, the apostle Peter wants to help them understand their place in God's economy and spur them on to holiness (1 Peter 1:13–16). He affirms for them, because they have been displaced and have had to be removed from their homes, that their inheritance in Christ is a permanent and imperishable inheritance (1 Peter 1:4, 18–21).

In the context of their imperishable inheritance, Peter gives them a command:

> Like newborn infants, long for the pure spiritual milk, that by it you may grow up into salvation—if indeed you have tasted that the Lord is good. (1 Peter 2:2–3)

Peter uses the analogy of an infant to stress to his readers the necessity of feeding on the Word of God. The word he uses, translated "long for," could also be translated as "intensely desire or seek." What parent has not seen firsthand the intensity with which a newborn will seek and earnestly desire his mother's milk? Without such a desire, the child would not live.

This metaphor of the Word of God as milk is used elsewhere in Scripture, and its use tells us something more about this "feeding process" with respect to God's Word:

> For though by this time you ought to be teachers, you need someone to teach you again the basic principles of the oracles of God. You need milk, not solid food, for everyone who lives on milk is unskilled in the word of righteousness, since he is a child. (Heb. 5:12–13)

The author to the Hebrews was concerned for exactly the same principles as was Peter; he was anxious to promote holiness in his readers. But he knew his original readers well enough to know that though they should be spiritually mature enough to be teachers, they had remained spiritual infants. They had not moved away from the elementary things of the gospel toward Christian adulthood (Heb. 6:1–2).

It seems likely that the plight of these Hebrew readers is similar to the plight of many in the Christian world today. It may very well be the case that there are multitudes of Christians who have received the pure milk of God's Word and perhaps have even (at least in the beginning) earnestly desired and sought that Word, but who have, for various reasons, been stifled in their pursuit of "every word that proceeds from the mouth of God."

What could be the reasons for this stifling? Surely there are enough specific responses to that question to fill a few books, but it may help us to focus our attention on a general trend or two.

With all of the time-saving technology and structures of convenience that have been built into our contemporary lifestyles, an objective observer might conclude that surely we have been given a life of leisure and contemplation that past generations could barely comprehend. In an ideal world, the savings of time and effort would translate, in the church, into Christians and churches whose knowledge and application of Scripture far surpasses that of our forefathers. But any perusal, for example, of John Owen's massive writings or the systematic theologies of our seventeenth-century forefathers immediately shames even the brightest and most prolific in the church today. How has this happened?

The easy and obvious answer is that this is anything but an ideal world. The more specific answer is that because this is a world infected with sin, those things that could easily do us good and provide occasions for holiness can just as easily take us captive and commandeer our best intentions.

It might be worth considering if our current time-saving technologies have accomplished their intended goal. Do we really find ourselves with ample time to relax, reflect, and meditate on the Word of God? The daily pace of our lives makes it difficult to simply "be still and know that [he is] God" (Ps. 46:10). Could it be that the only quiet minute in an entire week is the "silent confession of sin" that takes place in many of our churches? How is it that noise and activity have become the norm for us?

Could it be that the church is no less guilty than the culture in its attempts to entice us into the programming whirlwind? Some churches' activities list "opportunities for service" that begin on Sunday afternoon and continue daily through the next Saturday. This is not bad in itself; opportunities for ministry are opportunities for obedience to Christ. Of course, churches do not expect that every member or attendee will participate in every "opportunity." However, if someone wants to be "involved" or to "minister," some time and energy will be expended in finding just the right activity, right time, and right mix of people to meet the individual's and family's needs.

It may be that adding these opportunities and an abundance of church programs to the already hurried lifestyle of the average believer is not healthy emotionally, physically, or spiritually. The 24/7 busyness of our lives is not always a reflection of scriptural love and community, but instead adds to the detrimental effects of a chaotic culture, affecting both individual spiritual growth as well as the spiritual growth of a Christian home. Many of our schedules may not allow for casual reading, "easy listening," family time, or enjoying friends. Sunday, which is meant to be a rest from the daily grind of the other six weekdays, is now the major retail and entertainment/sports day in America. Perhaps we have forgotten what biblical rest is. Entertainment and busyness have been substituted for sitting at the feet of Christ and listening to his Word.

In his prescient and penetrating book, *Amusing Ourselves to Death*, Neil Postman explains one of the ways, perhaps the predominant way, that the technologies and time-savers of the present era have served to undermine those things that are deep and lasting. Postman argues that the exchange of the printed word for the entertaining image has caused western civilization to cease to think. Initially, Postman compares George Orwell's *1984* to Aldous Huxley's *Brave New World*:

> What Orwell feared were those who would ban books. What Huxley feared was that there would be no reason to ban a book, for there would be no one who wanted to read one. Orwell feared those who would deprive us of information. Huxley feared those who would give us so much that we would be reduced to passivity and egoism. Orwell feared that the truth would be concealed from us. Huxley feared the truth would be drowned in a sea of irrelevance. Orwell feared we would become a captive culture. Huxley feared we would become a trivial culture, preoccupied with some equivalent of the feelies. . . . In *1984* . . . people are controlled by inflicting pain. In *Brave New World*, they are controlled by inflicting pleasure. In short, Orwell feared that what we hate will ruin us. Huxley feared that what we love will ruin us.[2]

Postman writes with no Christian agenda; he is not interested in the impact of current technologies on the church, at least not directly. But as Christians we should ask ourselves, if Postman is correct, just what kind of negative effects might his analysis have on the church?

He gives an illustration (complete with a heavy dose of sarcasm) that might hint at the negative effects, even if inadvertently, of our entertainment culture on Christian truth and Christian living:

2. Neil Postman, *Amusing Ourselves to Death* (New York: Viking, 1985), vii–viii.

Not long ago, I saw Billy Graham join with Shecky Green, Red Buttons, Dionne Warwick, Milton Berle and other theologians in a tribute to George Burns, who was celebrating himself for surviving eighty years in show business. The Reverend Graham exchanged one-liners with Burns about making preparations for Eternity. Although the Bible makes no mention of it the Reverend Graham assured the audience that God loves those who make people laugh. It was an honest mistake. He merely mistook NBC for God.[3]

The point here is not that Billy Graham is particularly susceptible to such things. The point is that we all have been made susceptible to a predominance of the image—on the computer, television, movies, etc.—to the exclusion (or at least detriment) of the printed word. If this is true for Christians, then it portends a pronouncement of death. The exclusion of *the* Word for the church would mark its annihilation.

Postman's concern is that we recognize the negative effects produced when the printed word takes a backseat to the more glamorous, more colorful, but more superficial image. If we translate this concern into the context of the church, some important questions beg to be asked.

Could it be that, even in the midst of time-saving and convenient technologies, we are so influenced by the predominance of entertainment and images that we have lost our earnest desire to read and know *the* Word of God? Are there ways that the church has substituted entertainment and images for the slow, steady process of moving the Lord's people along from the infant's milk toward the meat of spiritual adulthood (1 Cor. 3:2; Heb. 5:14)?

---

3. Ibid., 5. Of interest to Christians is his chapter, "Shuffle Off to Bethlehem."

Whatever the reasons, the biblical mandate is clear. We need to be people who "safely feed upon the manna" of God's infallible Word. Our desire for intimacy with Christ must overrule and superintend any other desire, activity, thought, or action in which we are engaged, so that our longing to be with and like him becomes our controlling passion. It is the *Word* of God together with the weekly corporate *worship* of God that slowly but inevitably makes a spiritual infant into a mature and holy Christian.

In order to master this Word to the best of our ability, we have to set aside our (perhaps obsessive) penchant for images and entertainment as we listen carefully and reflectively to what the Spirit tells us in his Word. This Word has been given to us, like manna from heaven, by God's special providence. It provides for us all the guidance that we will ever need in this life. Properly and consistently used, it produces holiness in us.

CONCLUSION

If we are in Christ, then "this thing of darkness" has been transformed by the glorious light of gospel grace. That light now shines in us, exposing and overcoming the stubborn darkness that tries to remain. The Lord's illuminating light is present, always and everywhere. Nothing is hidden from him.

But he is *especially* present with his people, to guide, direct, provide for, and encourage them. His special presence and his "most special" providence toward us is calculated to move us ever more deeply and earnestly into the richness and beauty of his matchless Word. As we live, move, and have our being in the gracious presence of our Savior, who hovers round each habitation, his Word must begin to dwell in us richly. May we be those who steadfastly resolve safely to feed upon the manna of Holy Scripture, that we may be more and more like the One who grants us his presence continually and into eternity.

Safe they feed upon the manna
Which he gives them when they pray.

DISCUSSION QUESTIONS

1. How is it dangerous to believe that we are alone in the world? What is the only concept that can counteract this misguided ideology?
2. Robert Bellah argues in *Habits of the Heart* that the habits of Americans' hearts relate directly to our individualism. List some ways individualism affects your thought processes.
3. When the Lord promised to be with Moses as he led God's people to the Promised Land, what attribute of God is shown?
4. Men and women cannot hide from God. On the other hand, Psalm 36:7 discusses a form of hiding. What is it?
5. Why is there such disparity between our professed faith and our holiness?
6. How has the church substituted entertainment for the slow process of moving the Lord's people to spiritual adulthood?
7. On a scale of 1 to 10, with 1 being no desire at all, how are eager are you to read the Bible? Why?
8. How is the struggle to rest displayed in your life?

4: PAYMENT AND PUNISHMENT

WASHED IN THE REDEEMER'S BLOOD!

Bless'd inhabitants of Zion,
Wash'd in the Redeemer's blood!
Jesus, whom their souls rely on,
Makes them kings and priests to God:
Tis his love his people raises
Over self to reign as kings,
And as priests his solemn praises
Each for a thank-offering brings.

Narnia was under the reign of the White Witch. In Narnia, it was always winter, but never Christmas. But Aslan the Lion was on the move. And though the children were not sure just what Aslan's mission was, they knew that he was not going to let the White Witch do as she pleased. But then . . .

The Witch herself walked out on to the top of the hill and came straight across and stood before Aslan. . . .

"You have a traitor there, Aslan," said the Witch. Of course everyone present knew that she meant Edmund. . . .

"Well," said Aslan. "His offense was not against you."

"Have you forgotten the Deep Magic?" asked the Witch.

"Let us say I have forgotten it," answered Aslan gravely. "Tell us of this Deep Magic." . . .

". . . Tell you what is engraved on the scepter of the Emperor-Beyond-the-Sea? You at least know the Magic which the Emperor put into Narnia at the very beginning. You know that every traitor belongs to me as my lawful prey and that for every treachery I have a right to a kill. . . .

"And so," continued the Witch, "that human creature is mine. His life is forfeit to me. His blood is my property."

"Come and take it then," said the Bull with the man's head in a great bellowing voice.

"Fool," said the Witch with a savage smile that was almost a snarl, "do you really think your master can rob me of my rights by mere force? He knows the Deep Magic better than that. He knows that unless I have blood as the Law says all Narnia will be overturned and perish in fire and water."[1]

Though Aslan seemed the rightful ruler of Narnia, he knew, as did the Witch, that there was a "Deep Magic" that neither the Witch nor Aslan could overturn. What is this Deep Magic?

DEEP MAGIC

The "Deep Magic" of the Christian gospel refers, in part, to the agreement of the Triune God to save a people for himself—an agreement that took place in eternity past. In Christ's High Priestly Prayer in John 17, Jesus says that the work that he has accomplished on earth was the work that the Father gave him

---

1. C. S. Lewis, *The Lion, the Witch and the Wardrobe*, The Chronicles of Narnia (New York: Scholastic, 1995), 141–42.

to do: "I glorified you on earth, having accomplished the work that you gave me to do" (John 17:4).

The work of redemption—a work planned and accomplished by the Triune God—is a work that was planned and agreed upon before time began. This should not surprise us; all that God accomplishes in history has its origin and roots in eternity. The Lord is not surprised by the happenings of history. As the Lord, he rules history and oversees its events; he works all things by the counsel of his will (Eph. 1:11).

Though it may not surprise us, it should encourage us that God's plan for the salvation of his people is a plan that is grounded not in our response to that plan or in anything we might be able to accomplish. It is a plan that is grounded in the character of God himself and in the relationship that the persons of the Trinity have with each other. Toward the end of his prayer, Jesus says to his Father,

> Father, I desire that they also, whom you have given me, may be with me where I am, to see my glory that you have given me because you loved me before the foundation of the world. (John 17:24)

There are a number of glorious gospel truths in this one verse. We should note again that the realities of redemption in Christ have their origin and completion in the work of the Triune God, not in us. So, however much we may desire to be with Christ, what is even more dramatic, more decisive in God's gospel, is that Jesus desires to be with *us*. Jesus says in this prayer that it is his desire that those whom the Father has given him would be with him.

Being "with Christ," therefore, is something which Christ himself desires. It will happen not because we desire it first of all, but because *he* does. Could there be any firmer ground for our assurance? If Christ desires that we be with him, and the Father loved the Son before the foundation of the world, can there be any doubt that we will be with him for eternity?

MY SHEEP

Christ desires this, he says, for those "whom you have given me." Who might these people be?

As Scripture itself reminds us, those whom the Father gave the Son are the Lord's people. As the angel announced to Joseph, the child to be born of Mary was to be called Jesus because he was coming to save *his people* from their sins. Or, in Christ's own words:

> I am the good shepherd. I know my own and my own know me, just as the Father knows me and I know the Father; and I lay down my life *for the sheep*. And I have other sheep that are not of this fold. I must bring them also, and they will listen to my voice. So there will be one flock, one shepherd. For this reason the Father loves me, because I lay down my life that I may take it up again. (John 10:14–17)

The One who would save *his people* is the One who declared that he would lay down his life for *the sheep*. And who are these sheep? Jesus tells us how his sheep are to be recognized:

> Jesus answered them, "I told you, and you do not believe. The works that I do in my Father's name bear witness about me, but you do not believe because you are not part of my flock. My sheep hear my voice, and I know them, and they follow me. I give them eternal life, and they will never perish, and

no one will snatch them out of my hand. My Father, who has given them to me, is greater than all, and no one is able to snatch them out of the Father's hand. I and the Father are one." (John 10:25–30)

Note in this passage what Jesus does *not* say to the Jews. He does not say, "You are not part of my flock because you do not believe." That statement would be true enough, given certain qualifiers. But the focus of Jesus' discussion with the Jews in this context is on the work that he and the Father had planned in eternity. So, instead, he says, "You do not believe because you are not part of my flock." The *reason* that the Jews do not believe Christ is that they are not part of his flock; they are not part of those whom the Father gave to the Son.

The sheep for whom Christ lays down his life are those who hear the voice of Christ and whom Christ knows. They are the ones who follow Christ. The sheep are not an indiscriminate group out of which come the Lord's people. The sheep *just are* the Lord's people. And it is they for whom Christ died. Or, as Paul notes, Christ laid down his life *for the church* (Eph. 5:25).

Those given to Christ by the Father are those who were chosen *in Christ* before the foundation of the world (Eph. 1:3–4). They are the people of God, picked out from eternity and secured in the work that the Son accomplished in history (and which the Spirit *applies* in history). It is important to see here that the Lord's people are not simply a chosen people; they are a chosen people *in Christ*. In order for the Lord's people to be eternally *with* him, they must first be *in* him. And they can only be *in* him if he accomplishes the work that he agreed, with the Father, to carry out.

That work has its genesis in the agreement of the Father, the Son, and the Spirit before time began. In that agreement, the Son agreed to fulfill what Adam, and the rest of humanity, was unable to fulfill. He agreed to come down to the level of humanity (Gal. 4:4–5; Heb. 2:10–18). He agreed to submit himself to the law of God (Matt. 5:17–18; John 8:28–29; Phil. 2:6–8). He agreed to pay the penalty that the law demands, though the penalty was ours, not his (Rom. 5:18; Phil. 2:8). He agreed that the merits which he himself earned by virtue of his perfect obedience in life and death should be credited to those whom the Father had given him (Rom. 5:19; Gal. 2:20–21).

JUSTICE AND MERCY

There is, therefore, in this agreement from eternity, a perfect display both of justice and of love. It is not that God was able to overlook his justice and decide, instead, simply to love his people. This seems to be a common misunderstanding of what God is like. By some estimates, the only thing needed for an entrance to heaven is death. Since God is love, it is thought, he has a duty to forgive and to bring to heaven all who die.

But because God is altogether holy, he could not be God if he ignored or set aside those acts of sin that are rebellion against him. His holiness is in such stark opposition to sin that he cannot even look at it (Hab. 1:13). How, then, could he possibly overlook the sin that defines all who are in Adam? To do so would mean that God was unholy; it would be to demonstrate apathy (or, worse, agreement) toward those who break his law.

But neither is it the case that God's justice and holiness override his loving mercy. God, in his infinite wisdom, is able to demonstrate that both aspects of his character are a central part of his plan for his people. As a matter of fact, it is God himself who reminds us of both of these aspects in a key passage in the Old Testament.

The people of Israel had sinned by making and worshiping an idol, a golden calf. Moses' rage was such that he broke the tablets of God's law (Ex. 32:19). Moses intercedes for Israel, and the Lord's anger is appeased. Then, as the Lord agrees to be with Moses and with Israel, Moses blurts out a singular request, "Please show me your glory" (Ex. 33:18).

The Lord agrees to show Moses his glory, but only in its veiled form, "for man shall not see me and live" (Ex. 33:20). So, after Moses receives the law for a second time, the Lord tucks Moses in the cleft of a rock and covers Moses' eyes while he passes by. And as he passes by, he proclaims his sovereign character to Moses in what Martin Luther called "the sermon on the Name."

> The Lord passed before him and proclaimed, "The Lord, the Lord, a God merciful and gracious, slow to anger, and abounding in steadfast love and faithfulness, keeping steadfast love for thousands, forgiving iniquity and transgression and sin, but who will by no means clear the guilty, visiting the iniquity of the fathers on the children and the children's children, to the third and the fourth generation." (Ex. 34:6–7)

As the Lord passes by Moses, he reminds Moses, by repetition, that he and he alone is the Lord. He is the "I Am" who depends on nothing. He, and only he, is independent. Nevertheless, because he has chosen a people for his own, he is a merciful and gracious God, he is slow to anger, and he abounds in steadfast love. Here we hear from God himself that his character is altogether forgiving. Moses had just experienced that forgiveness as the Lord's anger against Israel relented at Moses' request.

But there is another aspect of God's character, affirmed by

God himself. Though he is merciful and gracious, it is not the case that he can simply forgive. His mercy and his grace do not eclipse or hide his justice. This "sermon on the Name" was given to Moses on Mount Sinai, the place where the Law of God was first given to Moses. That Law was given so that we might know how to please the Lord. Neglect of that Law, or a violation of it, surely displeases him. So, even though the Lord is merciful, he can "by no means clear the guilty." He must punish those who break his law, those who sin against him. And his punishment extends to every generation that continues to disobey him.

How, then, do these two aspects of God's character combine? How can a sovereign Lord, whose character cannot tolerate disobedience, at the same time be merciful? The answer to that question lies in the depth of the riches and knowledge of God (Rom. 11:33), a part of which is given to us, finally and completely, in the gospel of his Son (Heb. 1:1–3).

The sheer supernatural wisdom of this gospel should not escape us. Though it may be familiar to many of us, we should not lose sight of the fact that this gospel could only have come from the secret recesses of heaven itself:

> But we impart a secret and hidden wisdom of God, which God decreed before the ages for our glory. None of the rulers of this age understood this, for if they had, they would not have crucified the Lord of glory. But, as it is written,
>
> "What no eye has seen, nor ear heard,
>   nor the heart of man imagined,
> what God has prepared for those who love him"—
>
> these things God has revealed to us through the Spirit. (1 Cor. 2:7–10)

No man, no religion, has ever concocted a way of salvation that even approaches the glory and majesty of what the Triune God has determined "before the ages." We should be careful not to take the unparalleled uniqueness of this for granted. It is in this awe-ful and resplendent "good news" that we revel. This should help us see the glory of such an otherwise perplexing phrase, "washed in the blood."

Remember what the White Witch said to Aslan? "He knows that unless I have blood as the Law says all Narnia will be overturned and perish in fire and water." This was a central element in the Deep Magic, a magic that even Aslan could not overturn. Put in a Christian context, it means that "under the law almost everything is purified with blood, and without the shedding of blood there is no forgiveness of sins" (Heb. 9:22).

The Triune God determined what would be necessary if he were to save a people for himself. He determined what the law would require, given the entrance of sin in the world. He determined that "under the law" there is no purification or forgiveness of sin unless it comes by way of blood. For those who have been Christians for years, this language may be so familiar that its bleakness no longer affects us as it should. The reality of this verse, however, ought to strike us afresh.

Under any other circumstances, we would not think of blood as purifying us; to be washed in it would be repugnant to us. But, in God's plan, "the life of the flesh is in the blood, and I have given it for you on the altar to make atonement for your souls, for it is the blood that makes atonement by the life" (Lev. 17:11).

What does it mean to "make atonement"? Put simply, it means to avert punishment by payment. It does not mean to cancel or overlook punishment; it means that punishment is exacted elsewhere, on someone or something else.

THE DEEPER MAGIC

The Deep Magic includes the fact that those who are traitors, who rebel against the Lord, owe him their very lives and therefore belong to the "family" of the evil one (see John 8:44). But there is something that the White Witch overlooked; there is a "Deeper Magic." The Deeper Magic is that the Triune God determined to save a people for himself by way of a once-for-all sacrifice. That sacrifice would be of such a nature that no creature could duplicate it. It would be a sacrifice of the Son of God himself, in the flesh.

As we have seen, this is the focus of the epistle to the Hebrews. There the author is concerned to remind his readers that their hope lies not in the angels as messengers of God, nor in Moses as a mediator of God, nor in the Levitical priests as intermediaries of God. Their hope can only be in the Son of God himself (Heb. 1:1–3), who is the Great High Priest, and who, therefore, is greater than the angels (Heb. 1 and 2), than Moses (Heb. 3), and than the entirety of the Levitical priests (Heb. 5 and 7).

This is the Deeper Magic that was agreed upon and decreed before the foundation of the world. The lion, Aslan, explains this to the children. Notice what he says just after he has come to life following his death at the hands of the White Witch on the Stone Table:

> "But what does it all mean?" asked Susan when they were somewhat calmer.
>
> "It means," said Aslan, "that though the Witch knew the Deep Magic, there is a magic deeper still which she did not know. Her knowledge goes back only to the dawn of Time. But if she could have looked a little further back, into the stillness and the darkness before Time dawned, she would have read there a different incantation. She would have known that when

a wiling victim who had committed no treachery was killed in a traitor's stead, the Table would crack and Death itself would start working backward."[2]

This is analogous to Christ's substitutionary death on Calvary's cross. This is where the mercy of God meets the justice of God, as it was proclaimed in the "sermon on the Name" to Moses. It meets at the cross of Christ. There, at his death, a victim who had committed no treachery was sacrificed. His sacrifice was not for anything he had done. It was "in a traitor's stead." He was sacrificed so that we would not have to be. He was punished on Calvary so that those who trust him would not be punished, eternally, in hell.

The Old Testament sacrifices were meant to point the Lord's people to this one, great, and final sacrifice. For, while "it is impossible for the blood of bulls and goats to take away sin" (Heb. 10:4), Christ's own sacrifice for sins "perfected for all time those who are being sanctified" (Heb. 10:14). This is why there is no more need for a sacrifice. There was a time when the Lord's people, in order to please him, had to offer continual sacrifices to him. It would have been disobedient to refrain from these ritual sacrifices.

But the sacrifice of the cross changed all that. Since Christ's death, it would be disobedient to offer sacrifices to God; it would be equivalent to announcing that the work of Christ on the cross was not sufficient to save. It would be tantamount to an assertion that God's purposes for his people had failed.

But the message of the gospel is that God has accomplished his purposes in Christ. All the promises of God, from the beginning to the end of time, and into eternity, find their "Yes" in Christ himself (2 Cor. 1:20). When Jesus said, "It is finished"

2. Ibid., 163.

(John 19:30), he did not simply mean that his life was ending. He meant that the sacrifice of substitution that he had agreed to offer had been completed. The work required to cover our sins was finished. The Deeper Magic, arranged before the dawn of time, had been carried out in history. One who was innocent had offered himself in the place of many who were guilty. His blood would now cover their sins.

Mercy and justice come together at the cross of Christ. God did not have to arrange a way for salvation. He did not *have* to be merciful. By its very nature, mercy is optional; it is never required. But he did provide a way, a merciful and gracious way, that would also satisfy his justice. The blood of Christ was accepted as a satisfactory payment for the sins of his people. Justice was satisfied; mercy was extended.

THE GREAT EXCHANGE

It is important for us to recognize the cost of this justice. The cost was not simply in the *fact* of Christ's death. There is, at times, an undue focus on the physical pain and suffering of Christ's death on the cross. The physical pain and suffering were real and were a horrible part of what it meant for him to suffer and die on a cross. But much more horrendous, even unimaginable, was the *spiritual* pain and suffering that he had to endure to save us.

The apostle Paul describes Christ's death in this way: "For our sake he made him to be sin who knew no sin, so that in him we might become the righteousness of God" (2 Cor. 5:21). What could Paul mean when he says that God made Christ "to be sin"? He is describing here what has been called "the Great Exchange." In part what he means is that, in taking the sins of his people on himself, Christ became, at that moment, repugnant to his heavenly Father. No other explanation could be given for that great cry of dereliction from the cross, "My God, my God, why have you forsaken me?" (Matt. 27:46; cf. Mark 15:34).

It was not the pain of the nails that caused the Incarnate Son of God to cry out. It was that, because our sins were charged to his account on the cross, he was, in his Father's eyes—which are too holy to look upon evil—a disgrace. On the cross, the Father could not look at the hideous sin that his Son had become.

And Christ endured this heavenly desertion so that we would not have to. He took our sins and paid the price that we deserve, so that, as Paul says, in him we might become the righteousness of God. The Great Exchange that took place was the exchange of our sin, credited to Christ, and Christ's righteousness, credited to us, his people. As it has sometimes been put, "he became what he was not, in order that we might become what we are not." He became sin so that we might become righteousness in him.

We are, therefore, "wash'd in the Redeemer's blood." We are counted pure before the eyes of God because the sacrifice of the Son of God has made us clean. This is majestic and mysterious good news. It is, in fact, the ultimate good news, and is therefore the only good news that we truly need.

When we come to Christ by faith, the Spirit makes this good news *our* good news. He unites us to the One who gave himself in our stead. He gives us the eternal assurance that, once united to him, there will never be a time when we will stand outside of his pardoning grace. God has given us that greatest of gifts—himself (see Rom. 8:31–39). Once received, that gift changes us for eternity. Once received, we live our lives as those accepted by him.

KINGS AND PRIESTS

As those who are counted righteous in Christ, therefore, we are meant to live lives that reflect his. We are meant to be kings

115

and priests *under him*, so that we might reign *with him* and offer ourselves as sacrifices *to him*. But the Christian life doesn't seem to be that simple. Why not?

Charles Dickens begins his novel, *A Tale of Two Cities*, with the words, "It was the best of times; it was the worst of times." This phrase provides an accurate assessment of the Christian's life this side of heaven. There are times of great happiness and times of profound sorrow and sadness; times for both laughter and tears; peace and restlessness. We experience "abundant life," but also find ourselves waging war within the confines of our hearts and minds. Our thoughts wrestle and grapple with sin.

What does faith in Christ look like as we struggle against the powerful aspects of sin? John Newton reminds us that our souls rely on Jesus. We, the "blest inhabitants of Zion," are washed in the Redeemer's blood. To be washed in Christ's blood is to be cleansed of sin, freed from its bondage. That freedom is meant to give us rest (Matt. 11:28–30), and that rest has its focus in our attitude of trust and reliance in our Savior. So what do Christians look like as they rely on Jesus?

The Webster's 1828 *Dictionary of the English Language* defines "normal" as "according to a rule or principle." Definitions of this sort are often unsatisfying; they beg questions such as: Whose rule? By what principle? We would like to say that there is a common social standard for determining normal behavior. There are communication skills and social graces that make it easier to get along with each other, and most people adhere to these out of a need to feel accepted and to relate to other people successfully. Even these rules or principles change in varying cultures. But what does it mean to be "normal" mentally and emotionally? What rule or principle is to be used to judge whether one is thinking according to a normal standard? What does the normal Christian life look like and, just as important, what does it "think" like? Does the Bible give us rules and principles that define a normal Christian life? The apostle Paul, in the book of Romans, gives a description of the normal Christian life as he sees it.

Paul writes: "I do not understand my own actions. For I do not do what I want, but I do the very thing I hate" (Rom. 7:15). There are times we would much rather apply those words to our tennis game than to our Christian lives. It can be both funny and frustrating to think about our tennis game and our inability to make our bodies consistently do what we want them to do to win. How about life off the tennis court? It is still possible to think our actions humorous when we do things we don't understand.

In the spiritual arena, however, we should weep when we think about our inability to make our minds and bodies consistently do what God tells us to do. This struggle portrays the normal Christian life; sometimes we laugh, sometimes we cry. There are moments of peace when small victories are won, and there are periods of all-out war, when besetting sins lay siege to our lives. This life is neither characterized by sinless perfection nor total despair. We are not to live in arrogant antinomianism (attempting to live without reference to God's commands), completely ignoring God's Word and its guiding principles. On the other hand, we are not to live under brutal legalism, scrupulously attempting to keep the letter of the law, as if salvation depended on our works, and with no appreciation of God's grace.

SPIRITUAL CIVIL WAR

It can be tempting to simply look for a system of rules that spells out daily behavior and attitudes. Sometimes this can be a comforting set of rules and principles to define normal. However, we are not to react to this internal conflict with a deadening moralism that seeks to impose standards of behavior without reaching deeply into the human heart. An acceptable behavioral veneer, without connection to a deeper truth, is not the goal, or the "norm" of Christian living.

The Westminster Confession of Faith describes the process of sanctification, or the process of being made holy. The beginning of the chapter on this subject states that those who have "a new heart, and a new spirit created in them, are further sanctified . . . and they are more and more quickened in all saving graces, to the practice of true holiness." The second paragraph in the section concerning sanctification explains that because of the corruption still remaining in us, though we are being made holy, there will arise in the believer "a continual and irreconcilable war" (cf. chapter 13.1, 2). This continual war is a civil war between the flesh and the spirit, fought in the very depths of our hearts, and it is a "winner take all" war.

For a Christian, by God's grace, the forces that oppose our God-given desire to please him have already and ultimately been defeated; the warring factions within us are not equal in might. We can be thankful that the question of dominion has been settled. The problem, however, is that the world, the flesh, and the Devil seem to be unaware of the victory Jesus has secured for us

In Romans 7:14, Paul describes the current condition of the Christian. He writes in the present tense. He writes as a believer. Only one who knows both God's grace *and* his law could so honestly appraise his life: "For I know that nothing good dwells in me, that is, in my flesh. For I have the desire to do what is right, but not the ability to carry it out. For I do not do the good I want, but the evil I do not want is what I keep on doing" (Rom. 7:18–19). The sin that remains in the heart of the Christian permeates every fiber of who we are as God's children.

Satan can use this sin in us as he works to invade our minds and hearts. Remember the old refrain, "The Devil made me do it"? As much as we might like to shift the blame, the Devil and his legion simply stimulate the sin that is already in us. It is we, not he, who bear the blame for our own sin. Sometimes his flaming darts (Eph. 6:16) make small inroads into our thoughts and attitudes. Other times he stages "blitzkriegs" that can leave us exhausted and wounded.

The ironic truth is that it is just *because* our hearts have been changed that this remaining sin produces war. A heart that is only sinful will sense no tension in its perpetual disobedience. But since Christians are new creatures in Christ, the war rages. The Holy Spirit takes up residence in us, and his holiness militates against the sin that has yet to be purged from us. Such is the Christian dilemma.

This dilemma of the heart is like a country's dealing with two occupying armies, each fighting for absolute sovereignty. What is the source of this strife? Is it the law? No, Paul states on three occasions that "the law is good" (Rom. 7:12, 14, 16). Am I the source of the conflict? "Now if I do what I do not want, I agree with the law, that it is good. So now it is no longer I who do it, but sin that dwells within me" (Rom. 7:16–17). The "I" Paul is referring to is the new man in Christ who agrees with the law that it is good. So it is not "I" who wants to sin, but the sin living in me that does not do what "I" want to do. This civil war in the soul is the direct result of indwelling sin: "Now if I do what I do not want, it is no longer I who do it, but sin that dwells within me" (Rom. 7:20). Our being "in Christ" sets the stage for battle.

THE CALL OF THE WORLD

Our minds and dispositions are affected by this remaining sinfulness. We struggle to trust God. At times, his way no longer looks best to us. What if he does something with my life that is unexpected or that I don't like? What if it is God's plan for me to be sick or injured or poor? Is there not some way I can ensure security and peace for my future? How can I exercise some control over the pain and irritations of life? The flesh wants to be pleased, and the truth is that it can entice us to love and enjoy sin more than we love and enjoy Jesus. The sin that remains in us wants to promote a way of thinking that encourages us to be "lovers of self, lovers of money . . . lovers of pleasure rather than lovers of God" (2 Tim. 3:2, 4). And the unfortunate truth is that this internal struggle of the heart has its external supporters.

The world and the evil one work from the outside. The call of the world is not only the allure of material things and pleasure; those are merely symptoms of a deeper condition, a condition that tempts us to trust a philosophy of life organized and sustained without God. The Devil uses this philosophy to tempt us with all the world can offer—power, prestige, and every form of self-indulgence men and women have thus far imagined. The world explains our dysfunctions away so that we can excuse bad behavior or unkindness toward others.

The world's system provides educational philosophies and psychological coddling that work in direct opposition to the sanctification God is working out in our lives. The world presents theories and patterns for living that make us feel better about ourselves, even when confronted by our own sin. The evil one is a slanderer, an accuser, and a deceiver. He distorts the truth in at least two ways. On the front end of conflict, he leads us to believe that the sin we're protecting or contemplating will bear no consequences. Or we become convinced that we can fix the "sin problem" ourselves by appeasing God with promises of better performance, greater effort, or stronger endurance. As we come to understand our sinful thoughts and behavior and begin to look for God's help and forgiveness, the Devil throws the flaming darts of fear and doubt directly into our hearts and minds, convincing us that Jesus' sacrifice is not enough and that God cannot forgive us after all. Perhaps we don't even like the idea of a redeemer or a substitute. The pattern of the Christian life looks something like this: the more we grow and obey God's Word, the more sin we see in our lives; the more sin we see in our lives, the more we want to get rid of it and know God's forgiveness. The Christian life is a struggle for holiness; as Christians, in this life we are always at war. This is *the normal Christian life*.

MORTIFICATION

As we struggle to be holy, we are at war with sin. This engagement in warfare is sometimes called mortification. That word means to kill, to put to death. According to the Westminster Confession of Faith, "the dominion of the whole body of sin is destroyed, and the several lusts thereof are more and more weakened and mortified" (WCF 13.1). The desire for the philosophies and offerings of the world, the passions of the flesh, and the influence of the Devil are to be weakened and put to death in the life of the believer. The Westminster Confession of Faith refers to the "Spirit of Christ" as the one who gives a "continual supply of strength" in this war (WCF 13.3). It is by that Spirit that we "put to death the deeds of the body" (Rom. 8:13; see Col. 3:5).

Why engage in the battle? Why not seek convenience and comfort? We will never find the motivation to take on the task of mortification without the grace God has given through Jesus' sacrifice for us. Newton reminds us in this stanza of the hymn that we are "blest inhabitants of Zion." Zion is the heavenly city of grace, "the city of the living God, the heavenly Jerusalem" (more on this in chapter 5; see Heb. 12:22). We are blessed because we have been washed in the blood of Jesus. Our souls rely on Jesus because he is our Redeemer. As our Redeemer, he has paid our debt in satisfying the justice of God.

Daily, real faith in Christ looks like a battle. It feels like a battle as we struggle against the powerful forces drawing us toward sin like a magnet. Authentic faith is looking away from ourselves and looking to Jesus, "the founder and perfecter of our faith" (Heb. 12:2). He is the one who "Makes [us] kings and priests to God," according to the hymn. We reign with him, but we do so as we offer ourselves a living sacrifice (Rom. 12:1–2). The gospel changes our hearts; it comes from the outside in and causes us to engage in fighting the enemies that seek to destroy us.

John Owen wrote, "Mortification from a self-strength, carried on by ways of self-invention, unto the end of a self-righteousness is the soul and substance of all false religion in the world."[1] The active putting to death of sin, as well as our faith-response of repentance from sin, is the normal practice of the believer. Sin will never be totally eradicated, or mortified, from our lives this side of heaven. However, the daily practice of attempting to actively love Christ more than we love our sin weakens and mortifies the desires (lusts) of the sinful nature.

The war is fought by the consistent and deliberate rejection of anything—philosophy or activity, thought or emotion—that steals our affection for Jesus. This requires constant vigilance of the "eye-gate" and "ear-gate," turning away all enemies that compete for our hearts and minds.

1. John Owen, *The Works of John Owen*, ed. W. H. Gould, 16 vols. (Edinburgh: Banner of Truth, 1977), VI.7.

VIVIFICATION

However, mortification is not just a negative or corrective approach to the Christian life. The flip side of mortification is "vivification." If we put to death the deeds of the body, says the apostle, *we will live* (Rom. 8:13). Vivification is life in the Spirit. In weakening and killing the lusts of the flesh, our energies can be turned to setting our minds on what the Spirit desires. Loving worship and loving God's people, enjoying the sacraments of communion and baptism—all these positive and worthwhile activities can occupy their proper space in our hearts and minds when we cut off those things that lead to death. These life-giving activities become passions that will not drain and exhaust us, but give spiritual nourishment for keeping us strong in the battles we still face. This, too, is *the normal Christian life.*

So, the normal Christian life is not a battle in which we use a sniper's rifle to pick off sins of commission, staying safely behind the rocks and only coming out when we have a clear shot. The normal Christian life is not to be spent in constantly formulating new battle plans to include deeds we have omitted, so as to appease God's displeasure. It runs much deeper than that. Both of these examples envision negative, unhappy, mostly nonproductive pictures of Christianity.

How does the normal Christian life look on the outside? Newton writes in the hymn that we reign "over self" as king, and that we act as priests, bringing solemn praise to God as a thank offering. The battle has been won by Jesus' love. He has given us the power to reign over the sinful self with royal authority and status. Jesus has also made us priests to show thanks by our praise. So the normal Christian is one who has been given the power to reign over self—even if not consistently (Rom.

7:21–25)—and who is thankful to God for what Jesus has done. What is the disposition, the outward demeanor, the "tone" of our Christian lives? According to the hymn, there should be dignity and humility. Dignity is a pleasant attribute. Do our lives display a pleasant tone, a pleasing fabric? That pleasant tone is set by a heart attitude of humility worked out through self-denial at home, at church, and in the world.

Paul describes the warfare in the soul. He states that "the desires of the flesh are against the Spirit, and the desires of the Spirit are against the flesh, for these are opposed to each other, to keep you from doing the things you want to do" (Gal. 5:17). This warfare in the soul is to produce the pleasant fruit of love, joy, peace, patience, kindness, goodness, faithfulness, gentleness, and self-control (Gal. 5:22–23). This fruit marks the believer. The fruit is the very definition of self-denial. It provides a beautiful description of one who is dignified and humble. How can the noise and pain of battle on the inside produce beauty on the outside? The battle will not allow us to think of ourselves more highly than we ought (Rom. 12:3; Phil. 2). The battle will cause us to revel in Christ and his redemptive work more and more as we come to see the Spirit in us diminishing the presence and power of the sinful nature, the world, and the Devil.

This battle is the normal experience of life on earth. On the one hand, Paul sighs in defeat, "Wretched man that I am!" (Rom. 7:24). On the other, he answers his question, "Who will deliver me from this body of death?" with the cry, "Thanks be to God through Jesus Christ our Lord!" (v. 25). How does Paul move from defeat to victory? How does he live without condemnation (Rom. 8:1) and see himself in the assured position of being more than a conqueror in this near-relentless war (Rom. 8:37)? Paul knows himself and he knows God. He understands his sin and knows what God has done about it. God did not spare his own son, but gave him up for us all (Rom. 8:32).

We are able to see these passages vividly illustrated in the living and dying of believers. They struggle in the wilderness on this side of Zion; they struggle not to lose sight of that heavenly city, just across the Jordan. Though the blest inhabitants of Zion are here now, this land is not their home. We should never be too comfortable or content on this side of the Jordan. This is where the battles have been fought. The hope of Zion, in our hearts, has kept us going.

When we come to the end of our wilderness wandering, we want to die well. How? By understanding we are going home because the Redeemer's blood has paid for our entrance to that home. This thought is expressed so well in the old spiritual, "When I come to die . . . oh, when I come to die, give me Jesus."

So the normal Christian life is, indeed, a relentless war. If, ultimately, the victory has been decided, why can we not live in daily victory over sin? It is because our fallen flesh remains with us (Rom. 7:14–17), and it will not easily retreat. At the same time, the Spirit will not allow us to be comfortable with gratifying our fleshly desires. So "normal" Christians will find themselves on the front lines, earnestly endeavoring never to retreat, never to give up an inch of conquered ground to the enemy. "Normal" Christians may fall, they may be wounded, but their souls will never be destroyed in the battle. Why? Because of "Jesus, whom their souls rely on." The object of the normal Christian's faith is Jesus. It is not the believer's self-confidence, or simply faith in faith, but a reliance—even if small, weak, and fearful—on Jesus. The world, the flesh, and the evil one will never have dominion over the hearts of those Jesus is transforming into kings and priests to God (Rev. 20:6).

CONCLUSION

We are washed in the Redeemer's blood. He has paid all that is needed for the fullness of salvation to be ours. But salvation that is ours in this life is never as full as it will be. It is already fully ours, but not yet complete in us. Consequently, though washed, though fully forgiven, though counted righteous in the eyes of God, we are still involved in a lifelong process of killing the sin that remains, so the life that is becoming ours will be more fully evident. The salvation fully and perfectly accomplished in the Son is not yet fully and perfectly applied by us. In salvation, we are placed permanently on the road to an eternity with God in the new heavens and the new earth. But there are bumps in that road—bumps that are of our own making.

We pursue holiness, therefore, not as those who must satisfy the law's demands; Christ has already done that. We pursue holiness because the Lord who has saved us is pleased when we look more like him. We look more like him when we kill the sin that remains in order to live the life that he has given to us.

And as priests his solemn praises
Each for a thank-offering brings.

DISCUSSION QUESTIONS

1. How can God be merciful, gracious and just at the same time?
2. In John 10:25–30, Jesus describes how his sheep are to be recognized. What are the defining characteristics of the sheep for whom Christ lays down his life?

3. What is the "Deep Magic" described in this chapter?
4. The authors state that Jesus' spiritual pain was far worse than the physical pain He suffered? Why?
5. How valid is the phrase, "The Devil made me do it"?
6. What are the two main ways the Devil distorts the truth? Which one do you see yourself believing most of the time?
7. What is the civil war that is being fought in all of us?
8. Define mortification and vivification. What would mortification look like in your life? What specific areas would be affected?

5: SEEING THE UNSEEN

SOLID JOYS AND LASTING TREASURE

Saviour, if of Zion's city
I through grace a member am;
Let the world deride or pity,
I will glory in thy name:
Fading is the worldling's pleasure,
All his boasted pomp and show;
Solid joys and lasting treasure,
None but Zion's children know.

In the movie *Memento* (2001), Leonard Shelby wants to avenge the murder of his wife. The problem, however, is that Shelby has amnesia; he can only recollect events immediately present to him. Masterfully, the movie begins at the end. The audience is placed within the context of Shelby's amnesia as he works backward, using notes and other devices to try to find out just exactly what has happened to him and to his wife, and why.

As each mini-segment of Shelby's own experience concludes, it fades from memory just as quickly as another segment begins. In order to make sense of the end, which is where the audience, and Shelby, begin, we have to string together each of the mini-segments of Shelby's life until we reach the end of the movie, which is the beginning of Shelby's problems.

If this sounds confusing, it is supposed to. Perhaps no other movie has so successfully placed the audience into the mind of its main character. And because the movie depicts the experience of anxiety coupled with amnesia, the audience is enveloped into the handicaps of the main character. The chaos and confusion of his life is "lived out" by the audience, as well, as they seek, with Shelby, to make sense of it all. So successful is the movie in creating this experience, it is one of a very few movies that likely needs to be seen more than once.

Shelby's problem was that he was unable to connect his immediate experiences to anything else in his life. Each experience remained an isolated event, without context, cause, or connection, and so without interpretation or explanation.

In the movie, there is a beginning point of Shelby's tragedy and an end. What is most striking about the movie, however, is that both the beginning and the end play a minimal role in Shelby's experience. Rather, what the movie highlights is that Shelby's disjointed and seemingly disconnected experiences are all in desperate need of one primary thing—*explanation*. The reason things were happening the way they were was the goal of Shelby's pursuit. He, like the audience, was desperately trying to make sense of each of his individual experiences.

In that way, *Memento* is a countercultural movie. It goes against the now-common idea that our experiences are meaningful just by virtue of what they are. It points to the necessity of a *reason* for our experiences—a "why" and "wherefore"—if anything that happens "in the middle" is to be of any significance. Experiences cannot provide their own fulfillment or their own explanation.

In his book, *god is not Great*, Christopher Hitchens writes of the uselessness, even the *poison*, of religion (it should be noted that Hitchens is an equal opportunity despiser; *all* religions are poison, not just Christianity). He notes:

> Religion has run out of justifications. Thanks to the telescope and the microscope, it no longer offers an explanation of anything important. Where once it used to be able, by its total command of a world-view, to *prevent* the emergence of rivals, it can now only impede and retard—or try to turn back—the measurable advances that we have made.[1]

There is much here, and in Hitchens's entire book, however eloquent, with which we must disagree. For example, what we seem to have in this quotation is confusion about the meaning of the word "explanation." Hitchens thinks that, due to scientific advances, we are now able to *explain* such things as the origin of our species or the meaning of our lives, by way of the microscope and telescope. He thinks that because of these (and presumably other) inventions, religion has nothing really important left to say. Thus, religion has been neutered; it is no longer needed now that science and reason have progressed to their current evolutionary heights.

But what could Hitchens mean here by "explain"? Whatever he means, he seems to think the telescope and microscope have sufficiently replaced religion in their power of "explanation." He must think, therefore, that by looking at matters in more detail (microscope) or from a wider perspective (telescope), those matters will be adequately accounted for.

But this seems to be confused, if not naive. Haven't our advances in science raised more questions than they have

---

1. Christopher Hitchens, *god is not Great: How Religion Poisons Everything* (New York: Twelve, 2007), 282.

answered? Hasn't our exploration of the universe presented us with quandaries that seem to be irresolvable? Hitchens seems to think, to use an analogy, that one can "explain" the meaning of a word by more and more analysis of each of its letters. Or, he seems to imply that one can "explain" the meaning of life by learning more and more of the size and place of planet Earth in the cosmic expanse we call the universe. But this is, at best, misguided.

Returning to our amnesiac in *Memento*, just how helpful would the "telescope and microscope" have been for Shelby as he sought to fit the pieces of his life together to find the reasons behind his wife's murder? Why didn't Shelby, instead of attempting to "connect the dots" of his various life experiences, just go down to the local rental store and rent a telescope and microscope?

The answer is obvious in the asking. All that a telescope and microscope could have done for Shelby would be to *describe*, in more detail perhaps, his disparate and disconnected individual experiences. They could never have given Shelby the *explanation* that he needed in order to make sense of those experiences.

So it is with us. Even without amnesia, it is impossible to "connect the dots" of our life experiences without access to something that transcends them. If all we have are the experiences themselves, no amount of telescopic or microscopic analysis will give us anything more than "more of the same." Is there anything that can tell us not simply what our experiences *are*, but rather what they *mean* or *why* they are what they are?

One of the most pressing problems to plague western philosophy over the last few millennia is the problem of unity and diversity. In spite of philosophy's best efforts to keep such problems in the abstract, the fact is that this problem is one that confronts us all.

Heraclitus, a philosopher of the fourth millennium BC, is famous for his analysis of change. Because everything is in flux, noted Heraclitus, it seems impossible to make sense out of anything at all. Unfortunately for Heraclitus, *this* seems to make sense. If all we have is change and changing experiences, then any connection we might want between one experience and another is merely an illusion. Heraclitus's problem was Shelby's problem—he needed something that would *explain* the ever-changing experiences, but would not simply be one more experience.

The motivation to rise above our daily experiences in order to give them meaning is one embedded in us all. The passion with which so many embrace certain sports teams is one obvious example of this motivation. How do we get beyond the daily grind of our everyday workaday world? Why do I engage in this mundane job in the first place? Answer: *(insert favorite sports team here)*! What brings my experiences together and makes them meaningful is that I can champion the *cause of* "*x*" team. It is *the cause* that transcends the experiences of my day-to-day existence. So, even though the team's personnel or uniforms might change, my team being the best is what brings it all together for me. (So important is this for me that if my team is not the best, I may decide to inflict harm on someone or damage something.)

This is just one example of our attempts to bring together the disparate parts of our daily lives. There are others—so many others that the list could occupy us for some time. The same could be said of other, loftier, things: love and care for our families, raising the quality of life for others in some way (e.g., monetarily, medically), preserving the good gifts that have been entrusted to us, etc. These things can become *the* cause that interprets and explains everything else that we do.

The point is, we all strive to bring together those areas of our lives that occupy us every day. We try to bring unity out of diversity; we try to *explain* why we do what we do. We *explain* what we do by *referring* to something that rises above and beyond what we do. Such is the quest for meaning. It is a quest to make sense of our daily lives. It is a quest, sometimes more passionate, sometimes less, to rise above the daily grind and to commit ourselves to a cause.

SPIRITUAL AMNESIA

As we saw in chapter 3, the children of Israel were placed in the wilderness in order that God might test their commitment to him, the one who had saved them from Egypt. They failed that test.

Therefore, as the Holy Spirit says,

"Today, if you hear his voice,
do not harden your hearts as in the rebellion,
   on the day of testing in the wilderness,
where your fathers put me to the test
   and saw my works for forty years.
Therefore I was provoked with that generation,
and said, 'They always go astray in their heart;
   they have not known my ways.'
As I swore in my wrath,
   'They shall not enter my rest.'" (Heb. 3:7–11)

The story of Israel's history in the wilderness is a sad one and is open for all to read. The question for us is, how is it that they always went astray in their hearts? Why did they not know the ways of the Lord, especially after he had delivered them, guided them, and given them his Word through Moses? The answer, as simple as it is troubling, is this: spiritual amnesia.

Just after the children of Israel were brought out of Egypt (Ex. 12:51), we read, "Then Moses said to the people, 'Remember this day in which you came out from Egypt, out of the house of slavery, for by a strong hand the LORD brought you out from this place'" (Ex. 13:3). The command was clear. Israel was to remember what the Lord had done.

Memory is a mysterious thing. Philosophers have studied it; psychologists have analyzed it. Whatever it is, we all use it. We sometimes use it in a determined way, as when we memorize Scripture or when we study for an exam. Sometimes memory seems simply to "happen" to us, triggered perhaps by something else—some smell or song or occasion.

When the children of Israel are commanded to *remember the day* in which they came out of Egypt, they are commanded to use their memories in a determined way. They are to make sure that they call to mind exactly what the Lord had done in setting them free from Egypt, just how he had done it, and why. They are, in other words, to make sense of their current wilderness experiences by remembering the beginning (the Lord's deliverance) as well as the end (a land flowing with milk and honey).

But notice what happens:

Now the rabble that was among them had a strong craving. And the people of Israel also wept again and said, "Oh that we had meat to eat! We *remember* the fish we ate in Egypt that cost nothing, the cucumbers, the melons, the leeks, the onions, and the garlic." (Num. 11:4–5)

The children of Israel had been in the wilderness all of about two years. The Lord had faithfully guided them. Each day the Lord rained manna from heaven so that they would have plenty to eat as they traveled.

But notice in the passage above where the hearts of the Israelites are. Some among them "had a strong craving." They were focused on their own desires. The strong cravings that they had were not on the basis of anything they *needed*. The Lord had provided and continued to provide for their needs. But they had convinced themselves that the Lord, in fact, had not provided well for them.

Others of them began to weep. The inference here is clear. They did not weep out of real need or intense pain. They wept because they wanted things that they could not have. Instead of remembering the Lord, they said, " We *remember* the fish we ate in Egypt that cost nothing. . . ." The problem is *spiritual* amnesia.

But it is not simply that they have *not* remembered the Lord. It is worse than that. The problem is that they have chosen to remember something else, something *besides* the Lord. They have set their minds on things below, on their own wants, rather than on the salvation that the Lord has provided, including the gracious provision of their daily bread.

Spiritual amnesia, for Israel, was no small sin. It was the very rejection of the Lord who had saved them (Num. 11:20). At some point, there was a conscious effort on the part of the Israelites to remember—not the Lord and his gracious provisions for them, but the temporary and fleeting pleasures of Egypt.

The lessons for us are crystal clear at this point. Not only so, but the demands on us are all the greater now that we have what Israel could only look for (Luke 12:48; Heb. 2:1–4). We have the Lord's gracious provision in *himself* as the manna from heaven. Given that climactic provision, the question faces us even more pointedly—do we suffer from spiritual amnesia?

Do we, as those who profess faith in Christ, ever long for the food of Egypt? Do we crave those things that might provide temporary pleasure? A number of years ago, a survey was conducted to find out why, in the face of so much medical evidence, people continue their addictive use of tobacco. The answer was telling. The survey concluded that people were willing to exchange immediate pleasure for postponed pain. No truer conclusion could be drawn for the children of Israel in the wilderness. Instead of remembering their God and his gracious ways, they chose to remember other, temporal benefits. Are we willing to do the same?

This spiritual amnesia on the part of the Lord's people must have been all the more troubling to Moses. Who more than Moses would have understood the benefits of living in Egypt? Moses was a child of Egypt; he had been given great privileges there. But he saw such benefits as temporary, as distractions from his central task. Notice how the author to the Hebrews puts it:

> By faith Moses, when he was grown up, refused to be called the son of Pharaoh's daughter, choosing rather to be mistreated with the people of God than to enjoy the fleeting pleasures of sin. He considered the reproach of Christ greater wealth than the treasures of Egypt, for he was looking to the reward. (Heb. 11:24–26)

Moses understood that all that he had been given while in Egypt were "fleeting pleasures." He knew that *real*, lasting wealth could be found only in following his Lord, even suffering for his sake. To follow the Lord's guidance and commandments, even if suffering ensued, was prized by Moses more than all the treasures of Egypt.

Spiritual amnesia, by definition, looks to nothing permanent. It satisfies itself with "the fleeting pleasures of sin." Unlike

Moses, it has no view to the end; it does not look to the reward. It is willing to exchange immediate pleasure for postponed pain. It is a spiritual malady that can only end, like Israel, with death in the wilderness and no hope for the Promised Land.

We have been focusing our attention throughout this book on those spiritual realities and truths which can keep us from spiritual amnesia. Fittingly, Newton brings all of these things together in the last stanza of this wonderful hymn. He brings these truths together under two important and descriptive categories—*solid joys* and *lasting treasure*. It should be a fitting conclusion, then, to our present study to think briefly about these central aspects of our spiritual growth.

SOLID JOYS

In the second epistle to the Corinthians, Paul is forced to defend his own apostolic ministry. Though Paul contrasts his new covenant ministry with Moses' old covenant ministry (see 2 Cor. 3:4–16), there are similarities between these two ministries as well.

One of the most obvious similarities is that the apostle Paul, like Moses, is able to put his own suffering in its proper context. Unlike Israel, Paul does not long for days gone by and the temporal pleasures that were a part of the past. Instead, Paul understands, we might even say he *remembers*, "that he who raised the Lord Jesus will raise us also with Jesus and bring us with you into his presence" (2 Cor. 4:14). Like Moses, though Paul was "afflicted in every way," "perplexed," "persecuted," and "struck down" (2 Cor. 4:8–9), he was, nevertheless, looking to the reward. His mind was set on things above, where Christ is (Col. 3:1).

As Paul sums up his perspective on his own suffering, he encourages the Corinthians with these words:

So we do not lose heart. Though our outer self is wasting away, our inner self is being renewed day by day. For this light momentary affliction is preparing for us an eternal weight of glory beyond all comparison, as we look not to the things that are seen but to the things that are unseen. For the things that are seen are transient, but the things that are unseen are eternal. (2 Cor. 4:16–18)

This is the second time in this chapter that Paul says he does not lose heart. As with Moses (cf. Num. 11:11–15), the burdens of leading and shepherding the Lord's people have been almost overwhelming for Paul—*almost*. But Paul will not be overwhelmed. Instead, he remembers what the Lord has done. More specifically, he remembers the glory of the gospel as it is found in Christ:

Therefore, having this ministry by the mercy of God, we do not lose heart. But we have renounced disgraceful, underhanded ways. We refuse to practice cunning or to tamper with God's word, but by the open statement of the truth we would commend ourselves to everyone's conscience in the sight of God. . . . For what we proclaim is not ourselves, but Jesus Christ as Lord, with ourselves as your servants for Jesus' sake. For God, who said, "Let light shine out of darkness," has shone in our hearts to give the light of the knowledge of the glory of God in the face of Jesus Christ. (2 Cor. 4:1–2, 5–6)

Paul does not lose heart. He tells the Corinthians why, even in the face of intense opposition, he will continue his apostolic ministry. He will not be defeated or otherwise subdued by his present circumstances.

Why does Paul say that he renounces disgraceful, underhanded ways? No doubt it had something to do with those in the Corinthian church who were trying to undermine Paul's apostolic ministry. Perhaps Paul had been tempted himself to "fight fire with fire." Perhaps he had thought about countering the false teachers in the church by using methods just as deceitful as theirs (cf. 2 Cor. 10:1–6).

Whatever the case, Paul does not opt for spiritual amnesia. Instead, he remembers the glories of the gospel. He remembers that gospel not only for himself, but he remembers it *to* and *for* the Corinthians as well. He tells them why he preaches Christ and not himself. But in telling them that, he also reminds them that the preeminence of the gospel is theirs as well. "God," he says, "has shone in *our* hearts to give the light of the knowledge of the glory of God in the face of Jesus Christ." The light of the gospel, Paul is saying, is in all of us, because God himself has worked it in us.

But here is the irony that we as Christians must face. Any Christian will affirm that the gospel—its evidence of God's grace, its foundation in Christ's life and death, its benefits given to us by way of our union with Christ—is true. This means, at least, that what it teaches corresponds to what God has done and is doing in us, in the world, and for his church (Eph. 1:3–23).

The difficulty that we must face, however, is that this gospel—as Paul puts it, "the light of the knowledge of the glory of God in the face of Jesus Christ"—is, by and large, invisible to us. This is the irony. The irony is that the "solid joys" that only Christians know are solid not because we can physically hold onto them. They are solid because they, unlike the temporal things of this world, will last. In other words, the "solid joys" that are ours in Christ are those things that are invisible to us this side of heaven.

Paul makes this clear as he assures the Corinthians, for a second time (2 Cor. 4:16) that he has not lost heart. All that

Paul says in verses 14–18 he says because, in the face of much persecution and suffering, rather than grumble and complain and long for the "good ol' days" of the past (as Israel had done), he determines to remember the Lord.

So, says Paul, our outer nature—that which we see, which we identify in the mirror as "us"—is wasting away. The word Paul uses here is one that communicates a gradual downward process. Our bodies are on the decline; they are moving toward their inevitable end. Put in just this way, no sane person would deny it. The clear implication of this "wasting away" is that our "outside" is not the focus of our relationship to the Lord. It is, of course, *involved* in that relationship. Scripture elsewhere affirms that our bodies are not to be ignored (1 Cor. 6:13).

But our "inside," says Paul, is in the process of renewal each day. There is this invisible, central aspect of who we are that is in the process not of decline, but of growth. This decline/renewal process that Christians undergo gives Paul the proper perspective on his own suffering. Instead of complaining and grumbling about his suffering, Paul calls it a "light momentary affliction." It is light, of course, compared to the glory that will be revealed in us (cf. Rom. 8:18). It is momentary because Paul realizes that there will be a time when suffering will be no more. So, it is his remembrance of the gospel that determines how he understands his present experience. It is not the present experiences that determine Paul's perspective.

Notice here the solidity of Paul's language. This light momentary affliction "is preparing for us an eternal weight of glory." Here is the epitome of solid joys—an eternal *weight* of glory. In other words, a glory that will be "beyond all comparison." There is nothing in this life that could even compare to the weight of glory that is prepared and promised for those who have the light of the knowledge of the glory of God in the face of Jesus Christ.

But, lest Paul be misunderstood, he makes explicit what has only been implicit thus far. This eternal weight of glory, being prepared for us, is so prepared "as we look not to the things that are seen but to the things that are unseen." And why do we look to the unseen? "For the things that are seen are transient, but the things that are unseen are eternal."

Solid joys cannot ever be found in the things that are seen. By implication, solid joys cannot be found in the physical treasures and pleasures of this life. They are not found in the things that we see or touch. Those things, Paul says, are not solid, but transient. The experiences of life are in and of themselves unable to provide what we most need. These experiences come as quickly as they go. To understand the why and wherefore of these experiences, like Shelby in *Memento*, we have to know the why and wherefore of the end of the story.

Paul tells us that our why and wherefore is found in those things that are eternal; it is found in those things that are unseen. It is found in our invisible relationship with Christ himself, a relationship that has its focus and renewal, as Paul says, in the inner man. Though it takes place internally, it has its effects in the things that we do each day.

This is why, as Paul continues his thought, we are to "walk by faith, not by sight" (2 Cor. 5:7). The only way to see what is invisible, the only way to set our minds on the things above, the only way to have the eternal perspective needed to walk in a manner that pleases our (for now, invisible) Savior, is to walk by faith, to see by faith. The moment we focus our walk with Christ on that which is by sight, we move from "solid joys" to the transient, the disconnected, the temporal, and to that which is wasting away.

Israel complained against the Lord and his provision; they were sick of manna and wanted meat to eat. If we reverse the

Christian order, if we allow our external, visible circumstances to determine our relationship to the Lord, then solid joys will never be ours. Like Israel, we may receive some transient pleasure; we may get exactly what we want. But, like Israel, in the end it will make us sick (see Ex. 16 and Num. 11). Ultimately, like Israel, we will die in the wilderness, without access to the Promised Land.

There is another important dimension to "solid joys" that we should not pass over. We have been saying that it is those things that will not pass away, those things that are eternal, that alone can provide the "solidity" that we all desire. But, as we know, it is not bare solidity of which Newton writes.

He reminds us that those things that are "solid" are "joys." These are joys that are only ours because of our Savior. Again, the book of Hebrews points us in the right direction.

Just after giving us example after example of biblical "remembering" in that great Hall of Faith in chapter 11, the author concludes that segment of his discussion beginning in chapter 12 (why a chapter would *begin* with a conclusion cannot concern us here). Notice:

> Therefore, since we are surrounded by so great a cloud of witnesses, let us also lay aside every weight, and sin which clings so closely, and let us run with endurance the race that is set before us, looking to Jesus, the founder and perfecter of our faith, who for the joy that was set before him endured the cross, despising the shame, and is seated at the right hand of the throne of God. (Heb. 12:1–2)

We will remember that Paul sets before us the prospect of an "eternal weight of glory." In this passage, however, it is a weight of a different kind that is in view. Here, the author to the

Hebrews is concerned that we remove any sinful encumbrance, any sinful *weight*, that would keep us from finishing the "race" of the Christian life. The clear implication is that some sins, because of our failure to cut them off, can weigh us down due to our near-constant practice of them.

The language that the author uses here is intentionally general language. That is, it is meant to be applied to our own individual, specific situations. The author does not define for us just what the "weight" is because he wants us to take account of whatever it is that, for us, keeps us from running with endurance.

What is that "weight" for us? Perhaps it is a reluctance to trust the Lord in certain areas of our lives. Maybe we "allow" the Lord to be in control of our outward lives, but we refuse to give up certain deceptions of our own hearts. Perhaps it is our habits of speech; we may speak "Christian-eze" in church contexts, but we let our tongues speak all manner of offense in other contexts (cf. Rom. 3:14; Col. 3:8). It could be that the culture's perverse and soiled view of sex has gripped our hearts so that we think we are in desperate need of it.

Whatever the sinful "weight," it is a weight, says the author, that "clings so closely." The phrase used here can be translated either as an encumbrance or a distraction. The meaning is clear. In the context of a race, the weight of sin that we are to lay aside is that sin, or category of sins, that keeps us from running and finishing the race. These sins can keep us from completion because they weigh us down so that we cannot endure the race. Or, they can keep us from crossing the finish line because we take our eyes off of the goal in view. The point is that these are the sins that threaten to dominate, perhaps even overtake, our Christian pilgrimage. It is our Christian duty to identify these sins in our hearts and to lay them aside. To use Jesus' words, we are to "cut [them] off and throw [them] away" (Matt. 5:30).

It should not be difficult for us to identify these sins in our own hearts. The author writes with the understanding that each of us will know what sins so easily cling to us. Except in cases where we have allowed sin to bring us to utter self-deception, one look at our own hearts, with the light of Scripture shining on them, should be akin to one look in the mirror. We should begin to see ourselves so clearly that each and every blemish would be obvious.

The sins that seemed to plague the Hebrews were related to their struggle to persevere in the midst of persecution. But perseverance is not sensitive to context. Fighting the good fight of faith is difficult both in times of struggle and in times of relative ease. Those things that keep luring us away from that fight, that keep whispering that we should give up, and that seem to "make sense" to us, those are the sins that so easily entangle.

How is it, we might ask again, that those who have committed themselves to Christ and have publicly proclaimed that commitment can lead lives of privacy that are in fundamental conflict with the purity and holiness that honors the Savior? Invariably, the heart at some point loses its focus. We begin to convince ourselves that our lot in life is worse than it should be. We then deceive ourselves into thinking that we deserve better than what the Lord has provided. It is a very short though disastrous step, once convinced, to begin to provide whatever we think is "better" for ourselves. And what we think is "better" than what the Lord has provided is in conflict with his will for us. The sin that we orchestrate can then become a pattern in our lives. It can enslave us all over again.

Is it any wonder, then, that Jesus' language when speaking of such things is so severe? He does not mince words when he tells us how to deal with these sins. He does not say that we are to wean ourselves away from such temporal pleasures, making sure all the while that we are not too uncomfortable. He does not tell us to move away from them gradually. His language is clear. He says we are to amputate whatever sins remain in us and then destroy them.

How might this be accomplished? The author to the Hebrews, continuing his analogy of a race, gives us the answer. It is an answer that calls to mind what we have already seen. We are to "look to Jesus." We set our eyes on Christ. We remember the gospel, the good news. We see, in our mind's eye and by faith, what Christ has done, and why. As long as we focus our attention on him, there is no possibility of being disqualified from the Christian race. The Lord himself has finished the race in our behalf. Our great privilege is to follow him.

The author reminds us that this Jesus is the "author and per-fecter" of our faith. The translation here can obscure the point the author is trying to make, especially in the context of chapter 11. The phrase could be translated "look to the author and perfecter of *faith*, Jesus." If we are going to finish the race, we are not to look to the faith of the saints of old, many of whom are high-lighted in the previous chapter. Our eyes are not to be fixed on the "many," but only on the "one." Their faith, like ours, waxes and wanes. Instead, we are to look to Jesus and to *his* faith (see Heb. 2:13). That is, we are to imitate the trust that Jesus himself had in his heavenly Father (Luke 22:42; John 17; Heb. 5:7).

In looking to Jesus, we are to remember that in trusting his Father, he nevertheless was called on to endure the cross. The author is reminding us here that our trust, our faith, will undergo pain and persecution. There will always be, in this fight of faith, some measure of discomfort, even pain. But, as we endure, we should remember that when we endure, like Christ, it is "for the joy" set before us. The joy set before Christ, he says, was that he was exalted to the right hand of God (Heb. 12:2). We, of course, will not be so exalted. But, if we endure, the joy set before us is that *we will reign with him*: "The saying is trustworthy, for: If we have died with him, we will also live with him; if we endure, we will also reign with him" (2 Tim. 2:11–12). What is his *now* will be ours *then*, when we are finally and fully with him. And it will be ours for eternity.

Is there anything more joyful than that? To be not only accepted, not only adopted, but to be so united, eternally, to our Savior that his reign is shared with his loyal subjects is the height of joy for anyone who loves the Lord.

So, as Jesus himself taught us, we guard our hearts from the transient and temporal, and we invest ourselves, both inwardly and outwardly, in the lasting treasure of his kingdom. As Newton reminds us, the worldling's pleasure is fading. The pomp and show is only for a time. But if we belong to Christ, our path does not conform to the transient and fading. Instead:

> Do not lay up for yourselves treasures on earth, where moth and rust destroy and where thieves break in and steal, but lay up for yourselves treasures in heaven, where neither moth nor rust destroys and where thieves do not break in and steal. For where your treasure is, there your heart will be also. (Matt. 6:19–21)

ZION'S CHILDREN

Solid joys and lasting treasure, none but Zion's children know. But what does it mean for us to be "Zion's children"? What does it mean for us through grace to be a member of "Zion's city"? Perhaps the passage that fittingly brings our discussion to a close is found in the book of Hebrews, toward the end of chapter 12. There, beginning in verse 18, the author gives us another contrast between that which is temporal, transient, and "touched" and that which is eternal—between "things that are

147

shaken," things that "have been made" and "things that cannot be shaken" and that "remain" (v. 27).

The contrast that we have in the book of Hebrews between that which is temporal and fleeting and that which is eternal and solid has its focus in the differences between the new covenant in Christ and the old covenant. In that way, the context in which the epistle is written is different from ours.

The principles given to us, however, are the same. Just as the original readers of Hebrews were to leave behind their old ways and look to Christ, so also are we. Just as they were encouraged to "strive for . . . holiness without which no one will see the Lord" (v. 14), so also are we.

The final, climactic contrast that the author offers his readers is that between Mount Sinai, and all that it represented under the old covenant, and Mount Zion, and all that it represents under the new covenant in Christ. To put the contrast in its most general terms, it is between those things that could be seen, touched, and heard (those things that are temporary) and those things that are permanent and invisible, on the other hand. In that way, the following passage aptly summarizes the substance of all of our discussions to this point:

> But you have come to Mount Zion and to the city of the living God, the heavenly Jerusalem, and to innumerable angels in festal gathering, and to the assembly of the firstborn who are enrolled in heaven, and to God, the judge of all, and to the spirits of the righteous made perfect, and to Jesus, the mediator of a new covenant, and to the sprinkled blood that speaks a better word than the blood of Abel. (Heb. 12:22–24)

Here, the author echoes what Newton surely must have been thinking. He sees us as citizens of Zion. The reason for this, as for much of what is written in Hebrews (since it was written, originally, to *Hebrews*), is the rich historical, old covenant background of the audience.

The word "Zion" to a Hebrew would have conjured up the same ideas as the word "heaven" conjures up for us. As we have seen, Zion, in the Old Testament, was equivalent to Jerusalem; it was the city of David (2 Sam. 5:7; 1 Kings 8:1; 1 Chron. 11:5; 2 Chron. 5:2; Ps. 48:1–2). Zion is the place where God would complete his plan for his people. "For a people shall dwell in Zion, in Jerusalem; you shall weep no more" (Isa. 30:19). "Great is the LORD and greatly to be praised in the city of our God! His holy mountain, beautiful in elevation, is the joy of all the earth, Mount Zion, in the far north, the city of the great King" (Ps. 48:1–2). Clearly, Zion was the place of God's final resting place with his people.

The author to the Hebrews wants his readers to understand that, because of Christ our great High Priest, those whose faith is in him *have already come* to the Great Mountain. The transition from the fear and trembling of Mount Sinai, wherein a judgment awaits those who break the law of God, to praise and worship on Mount Zion, where grace brings joy and celebration—that transition—is not one that is wholly future. It is a transition that takes place immediately for those who have set their eyes on Jesus.

Since that transition is present as well as future, we are reminded again that the joy, the worship, the celebration, and the gratitude all have their focus in that which is invisible. They have their center in "a kingdom that cannot be shaken" (Heb. 12:28). This kingdom is "the city of the living God, the heavenly Jerusalem" (12:22). In that city are "innumerable angels in festal gathering" as well as the "assembly of the firstborn who are enrolled in heaven" (12:22, 23). The "spirits of the righteous made perfect" (12:23) are there.

Most importantly, there, in Zion, is "God, the judge of all" (12:23) and "Jesus, the mediator of a new covenant" (12:24). All of these aspects to the kingdom, which is now ours and is also coming in the future, are those things that are not seen, those eternal things that will one day be revealed to us.

But just *where* is this Zion? The point the author is making is that Zion, the city of the Great King, is *here*; it is wherever those who are its citizens reside. Or, to put it in Paul's terms, it is not only that Zion is *here*, but it is that we who have come to Christ are citizens *there*.

In his explanation of salvation in Ephesians 2:4–6, the apostle Paul makes it plain that we have been saved by grace, through faith. But he also makes plain what the *effect* of that salvation is. God has not only saved us by grace through faith, but he has also "raised us up with him and *seated us with him* in the heavenly places in Christ Jesus" (Eph. 2:6).

The reason, therefore, that "we have come to Mount Zion" is because God has first come to us in Christ. And the reason that Mount Zion is *here* is because, in Christ, we are *there*. Our citizenship is in heaven (Phil. 3:20); if we have trusted Christ, we belong to an eternal city, a city whose builder is God and that God has prepared for those who love him (Heb. 11:10,16). That city is finally and climactically finished when Christ comes back, but it is just as real now as it will be then. We, *right now*, belong to that city—the city that alone has an eternal foundation.

As we saw earlier, virtually every age has to deal with change and its consequences. The original readers of the epistle to the Hebrews were having difficulty adjusting their own notions of what they knew about Christ with their past. They were in danger of neglecting the benefits that they had received in Christ. So dangerous was their neglect that the author has to warn them repeatedly of its eternal dangers (see, for example, Heb. 2:1–4; 6:1–6; 10:26–31; 12:25–26).

As those who name the name of Christ, we have the responsibility—indeed the great privilege—of setting our hearts and minds on those things that are eternal, things that cannot be shaken. If we, like the prodigal son, desire to return to the pig slop of our past, we will be investing our lives in those things that are temporal, and our reward will be just as fleeting.

It is, by God's grace, our faith in Christ that will need to be strong to endure whatever may come. Only the perspective of faith can provide what is needed in the face of temptations that come our way. Even as Noah's faith allowed him to see the invisible, so that he, in "reverent fear," was obedient to his Lord (Heb. 11:7), so in our gratitude we are to "offer to God acceptable worship, with reverence and awe" (Heb. 12:28). Unlike Noah, who looked forward to the fulfillment of God's promises, we have seen the "yes" and "amen" of all the promises of God in Christ (2 Cor. 1:20).

CONCLUSION

The change around us, whatever its content, is only for a time. It is not designed to give us fulfillment. It surely cannot provide meaning to the experiences of our daily lives. Those experiences themselves are transient; they come and go with the times. If we are intent on pleasing the One who has delivered us from our slavery to sin, we must, each day, put our trust in him. Faith is the prerequisite for pleasing God (Heb. 11:6). It is that faith that should issue forth in gratitude and worship. In gratitude and worship, we place ourselves squarely within the center of God's kingdom, and we hold fast to him.

Do you know these things that cannot be shaken? Are you a

citizen of Zion, so that solid joys and lasting treasure are yours, both now and forever? If you are in Christ, by grace through faith, then you now reside with him in the heavenlies. Solid joys are yours; lasting treasure is within your grasp. They can only be had by those who refuse to wed themselves to the spirit of the age. They belong to those who are guided by that which cannot be seen, and which is eternal.

That which is invisible now will one day be visible. Those things that we see now with the eyes of faith will one day be presented to us by sight. This life, in which we are called on to "see" the invisible, is our preparation for the life to come, when the invisible will be visible, for eternity. We live by faith *here*, that we may live, for eternity, by sight *there*.

Lewis provides a typically memorable analogy to this. In *The Voyage of the Dawn Treader*, the children, Edmund and Lucy, are about to leave the land of Narnia:

"Please, Aslan," said Lucy. "Before we go, will you tell us when we can come back to Narnia again? Please. And oh, do, do, do make it soon."

"Dearest," said Aslan very gently, "you and your brother will never come back to Narnia."

"Oh, *Aslan*!" said Edmund and Lucy both together in despairing voices.

"You are too old, children," said Aslan, "and you must begin to come close to your own world now."

"It isn't Narnia, you know," sobbed Lucy. "It's *you*. We shan't meet *you* there. And how can we live, never meeting you?"

"But you shall meet me, dear one," said Aslan.

"Are—are you there too, Sir?" said Edmund.

"I am," said Aslan. "But there I have another name. You must learn to know me by that name. This was the very reason why you were brought to Narnia, that by knowing me here for a little, you may know me better there."[1]

We are now, as it were, in Narnia. As we know Christ *here*, more and more, we are preparing ourselves to know him better *there*, where he will have a new name (Rev. 3:12; cf. Rev. 19:11–16). There we will see him face to face, and his presence, now invisible to us, will be visible in all its glory. On that day, all those invisible things that seemed so elusive to us at times, on earth, will become visible. Because of that visible presence, we will be forever fully sanctified and fully glorified. At that time, our eternal lives will consist of nothing but "solid joys and lasting treasure." Those "things which cannot be shaken" which are ours *here* will also be ours for eternity *there*.

Beloved, we are God's children now,
and what we will be has not yet appeared;
but we know that when he appears we shall be like him,
because we shall see him as he is.
And everyone who thus hopes in him
purifies himself as he is pure. (1 John 3:2–3)

DISCUSSION QUESTIONS

1. "The motivation to rise above our daily experiences in order to give them meaning is one embedded in us all." What are you passionate about that allows you to keep going day after day?

1. C. S. Lewis, *The Voyage of the Dawn Treader*, The Chronicles of Narnia (New York: Collier, 1972), 215–16.

2. What is Christopher Hitchens's main assertion about religion?
3. What is spiritual amnesia? Have there been moments you have forgotten the good things God has done in your life? Who are you?
4. What is a weight that keeps you from running with endurance?
5. What would be worse than forgetting God's providence and his mercy?
6. How have you focused your life in Christ, wrongly, on things that are seen rather than things that are unseen?
7. What are the solid joys a believer counts on? Where are these solid joys found?
8. What would you consider to be the most significant solid joy in your life?
9. What aspects of the kingdom give us hope for the future?

MORE FROM P&R ON JOHN NEWTON

Barbara Duguid turns to the writings of John Newton to teach us God's purpose for our failure and guilt—and to help us adjust our expectations of ourselves. Her empathetic, honest approach lifts our focus from our own performance back to the God who is bigger than our failures—and who uses them for his glory. Rediscover how God's extravagant grace makes the gospel once again feel like the good news it truly is!

"Take this book to heart. It will sustain you for the long haul, long after the hyped-up panaceas and utopias fail."
—**David Powlison,** Faculty Member at the Christian Counseling and Educational Foundation

"Barb tells the story of God's unrelenting compassion toward sinners like us with profound wisdom."
—**Michael S. Horton**, J. Gresham Machen Professor of Systematic Theology and Apologetics, Westminster Seminary California

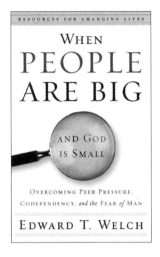

"Need people less. Love people more. That's the author's challenge. . . . He's talking about a tendency to hold other people in awe, to be controlled and mastered by them, to depend on them for what God alone can give. . . . [Welch] proposes an antidote: the fear of God . . . the believer's response to God's power, majesty and not least his mercy."

   —*Dallas Morning News*

"Refreshingly biblical . . . brimming with helpful, readable, practical insight."

   —**John MacArthur,** President of The Master's College and
      Seminary

"Ed Welch is a good physician of the soul. This book is enlightening, convicting, and encouraging. I highly recommend it."

   —**Jerry Bridges,** Author of *Trusting God*

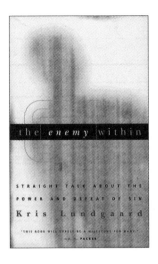

This book takes dead aim at the heart of ongoing sin. Drawing from two masterful works by John Owen, Kris Lundgaard offers insight, encouragement, and hope for overcoming the enemy within.

"A solid reminder that apart from the grace of God we are far weaker than we can imagine—but greater is he that is in us than he that is in the world."
    —**Bryan Chapell,** Author of *Holiness by Grace: Delighting in the Joy That Is Our Strength*

"Fresh, contemporary, highly readable. Every Christian who is serious about holiness should read this book."
    —**Jerry Bridges,** Author of *Respectable Sins: Confronting the Sins We Tolerate*